MAO
FOR BEGINNERS™

Rius and friends

Illustrated by
Rius and friends

Orient BlackSwan

MAO FOR BEGINNERS

ORIENT BLACKSWAN PRIVATE LIMITED

Registered Office
3-6-752 Himayatnagar, Hyderabad 500 029 (A.P.), INDIA
e-mail: centraloffice@orientblackswan.com

Other Offices
Bangalore, Bhopal, Bhubaneshwar, Chennai, Ernakulam, Guwahati, Hyderabad, Jaipur, Kolkata, Lucknow, Mumbai, New Delhi, Patna

Cover Design: Susetta Bozzi

Published by arrangement with
Writers and Readers Limited
P O Box 29522
London N1 8 FB

First published in India by
Orient Longman Private Limited 2002
Reprinted 2006
First Orient Blackswan impression 2010

ISBN 13: 978 81 250 2235 0
ISBN 10: 81 250 2235 X

Printed in India at
Yash Printographics
Noida

Published by
Orient Blackswan Private Limited
1/24 Asaf Ali Road
New Delhi 110 002
e-mail: delhi@orientblackswan.com

MAO
FOR BEGINNERS

by Rius and friends

The Author extends his thanks to:
Tom Engelhardt, Jim Peck, Richard Appignanesi, Maria Clarkson, Frances Wood, Malcolm Smythe, Lee Robinson, Brian Dax, Safu-Maria Gilbert, Tim Spengler, John King, Bread 'n' Roses and Book Services Limited.
and Gubbins for 11th-hour artwork!
(eat your heart out, Gonzo!)

A revolution is not a dinner party, or writing an essay, or painting a picture, or doing embroidery; it cannot be so refined, so leisurely and gentle, so temperate, kind, courteous, restrained and magnanimous. A revolution is an insurrection, an act of violence by which one class overthrows another.

Mao Tsetung, 1927

So much cries out to be done
And always urgently.
The world rolls on,
Time presses.
Ten thousand years are too long,
Now is the time!

from Mao's poem, *Reply to Kuo Mojo*, 1963.

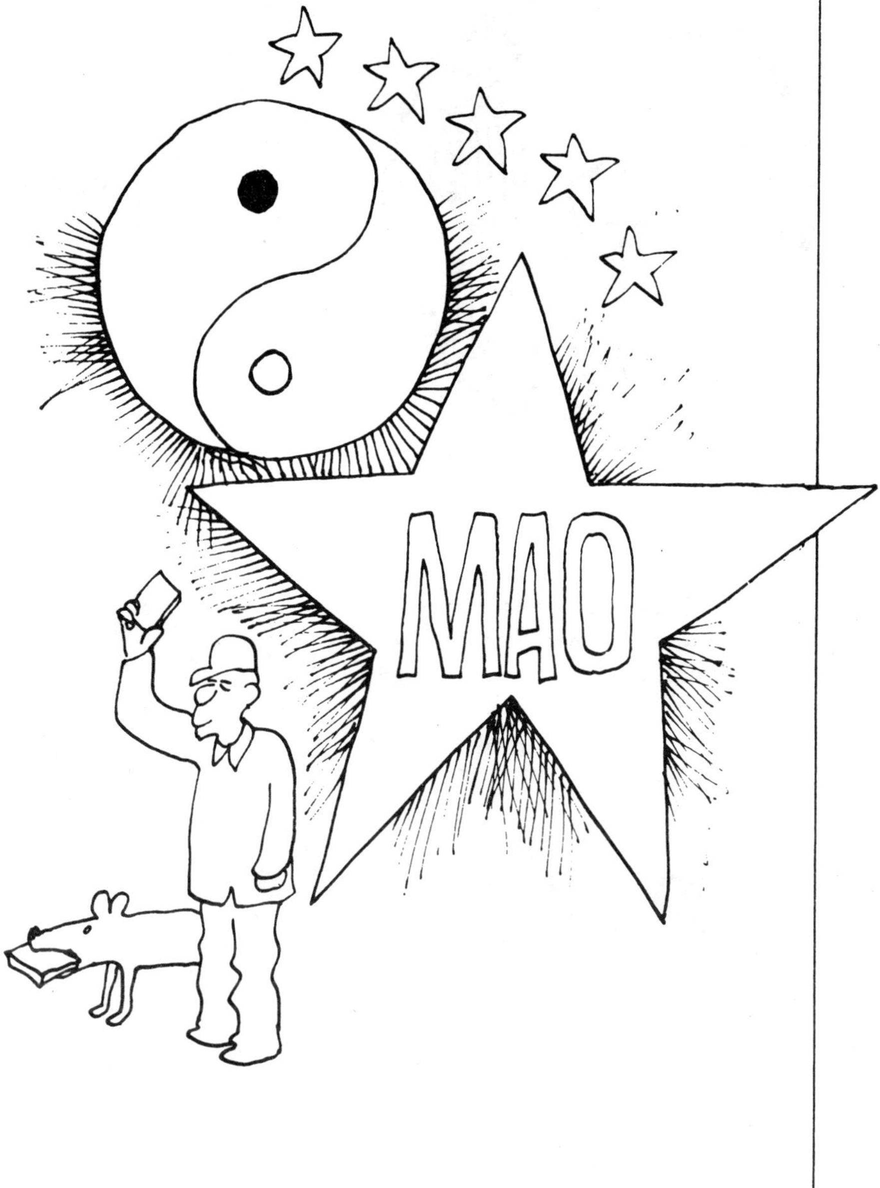

The story of Mao Tsetung is the story of Modern China. If Mao hadn't existed there would be no People's Republic of China today. Though Mao would have said that it was thanks to the Communist Party and the brave peasants that China was liberated, not thanks to him . . .

MAO, the eldest of four children, was born on 26 December 1893 in the village of Shao Shan, Hunan province.

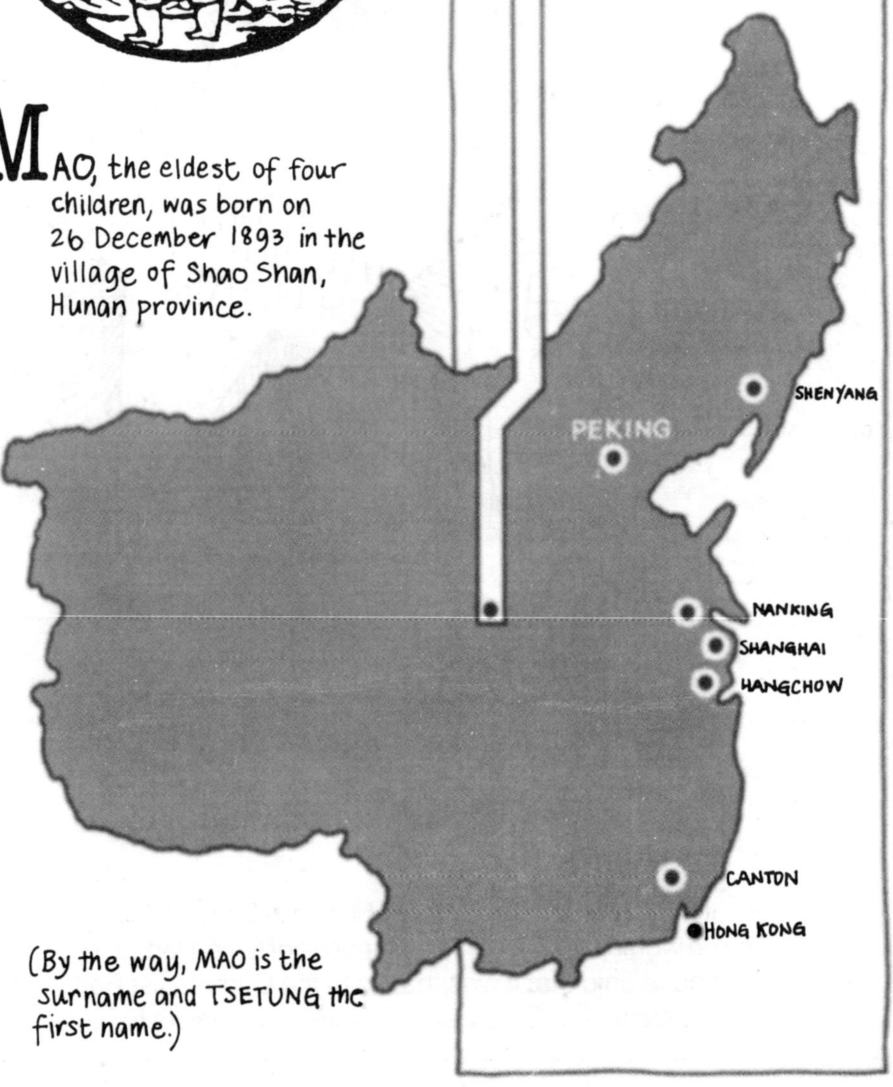

(By the way, MAO is the surname and TSETUNG the first name.)

ACCORDING to chinese astrology, Mao Tse tung was born in the year of the Black Snake, in the hour of the Green Dragon, sign of a life destined for blood and violence, and great victories alternating with humiliating compromises.

"My father was a poor peasant and while still young was obliged to join the army because of heavy debts. He was a soldier for many years. Later on he returned to the village where I was born, and by saving carefully and gathering together a little money through small trading and other enterprise he managed to buy back his land."

from Edgar Snow, *Red Star over China*

Mao (right) with some of his family

ACCORDING to Confucian tradition, a girl was married off to a man of her parent's choice and then became the slave of her parents-in-law, of her husband, and even her son.

Mao's mother was no exception to that school of thought.

But Mao did not follow the Confucian tradition of filial piety....

"There were two parties in the family. One was my father, the Ruling Power. The Opposition was made up of myself, my mother, my brother."

Traditionally, the people of Hunan were known as rebels and bandits.

Uprisings were savagely repressed by the local bureaucrats. When he was at school, Mao saw the decapitated heads of peasant rebels stuck up on the city gates as a warning. They had led starving peasants to find food...

"This incident was discussed in my school for many days. It made a deep impression on me. Most of the other students sympathized with the 'insurrectionists,' but only from an observer's point of view. They did not understand that it had any relation to their own lives. They were merely interested in it as an exciting incident. I never forgot it. I felt that there with the rebels were ordinary people like my own family and I deeply resented the injustice of the treatment given to them."

From '*RED STAR OVER CHINA*'

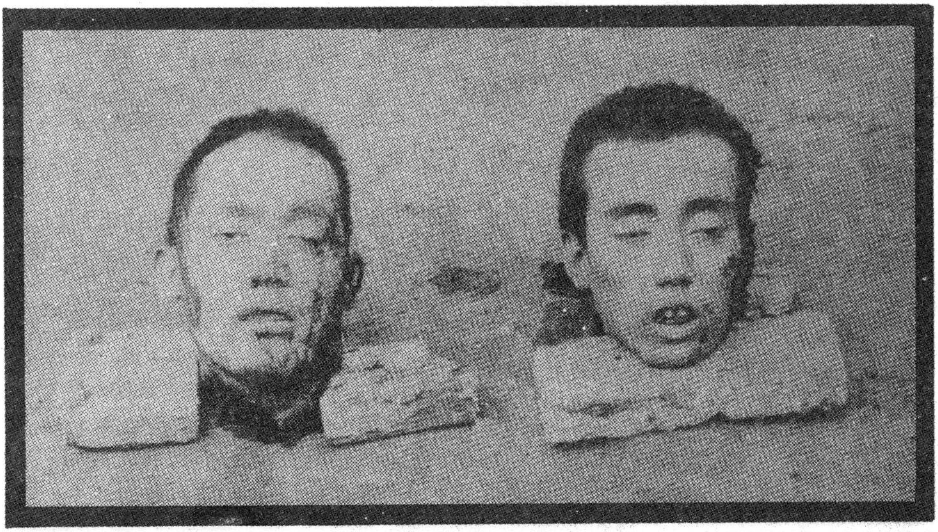

Mao was a young rebel. He was unwilling to accept orders. He didn't want to keep accounts for his father or be an apprentice in a rice shop. He preferred reading romantic stories of old China, like *The Water Margin*, or chatting with the peasants.

Not at all. Mao's father wanted him to know the Confucian Classics. Mao's father had once been defeated in a lawsuit because of an "apt Classical quotation used by his adversary in the Chinese court". So the Classics were practical! But Mao rebelled.

So, what's the big mystery of Chin

NO MYSTERY, only the long history of an exploited people. Mao saw it. His peasant background also provided him with a belief: "Whoever wins the peasants will win China. Whoever solves the land problem will win the peasants."

Street beggars – a common sight in old China!

Against his father's wishes, but with his mother's support, Mao left home at 16 to study at a radical new school, the Xinjiang Institute. There he learned about the history of his country.

China was, even in the 20th century, a feudal-bureaucratic country. At the top of the power pyramid sat the Emperor, served by thousands of local officials who extorted grain tax from the starving peasants. Peasants were at the bottom of the pyramid, oppressed both by the landlord and bureaucrats. The ideology of this ruling class was Confucianism, whose voluminous "Classics" were used to justify the workings of society. Landlords bought an education and official positions for their sons. Bureaucrats bought land as an economic bolster to their government positions.

a?

"Great men have their proper business, and little men have their proper business..."

"Some labor with their minds, and some labor with their strength. Those who labor with their minds govern others; those who labor with their strength are governed by others. Those who are governed by others support them; those who govern others are supported by them."

MENCIUS (372–289 B.C.) Confucian philosopher and literary gent

Peasants had struggled against this system for centuries.

But they were always crushed.

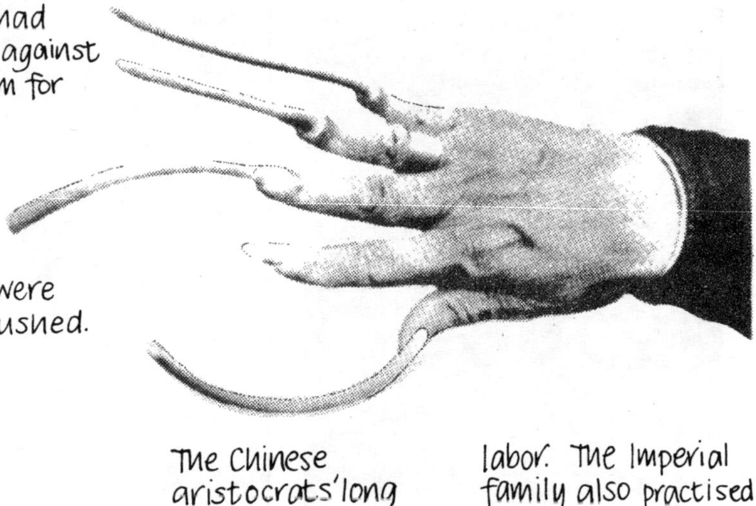

The Chinese aristocrats' long nails showed that they did no manual labor. The Imperial family also practised this weird and wonderful exercise!

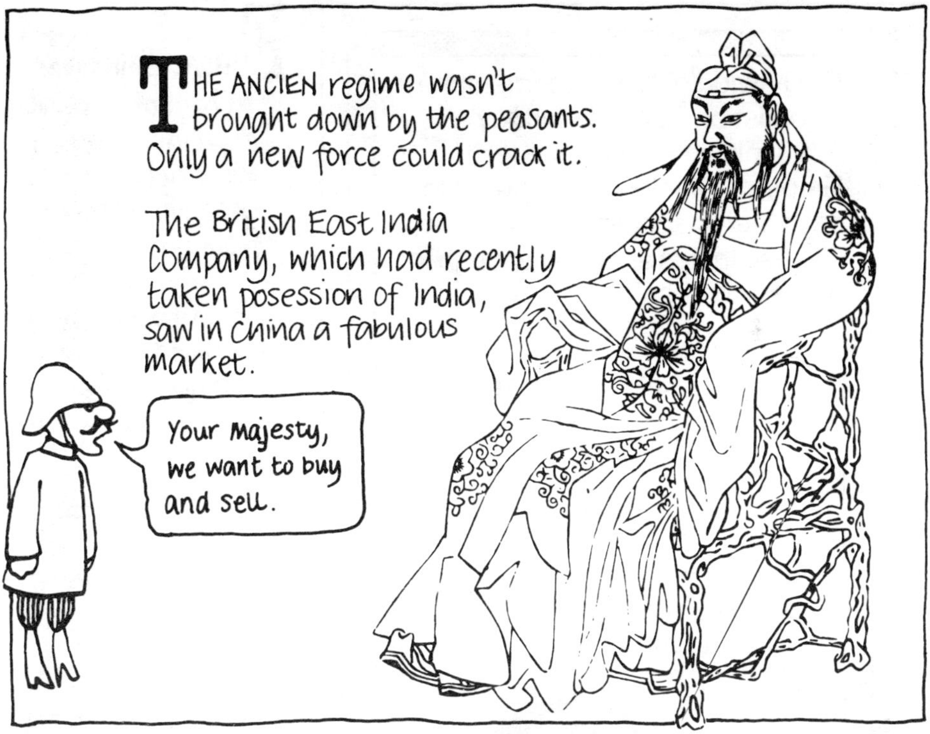
THE ANCIEN regime wasn't brought down by the peasants. Only a new force could crack it.
The British East India Company, which had recently taken posession of India, saw in China a fabulous market.
Your majesty, we want to buy and sell.

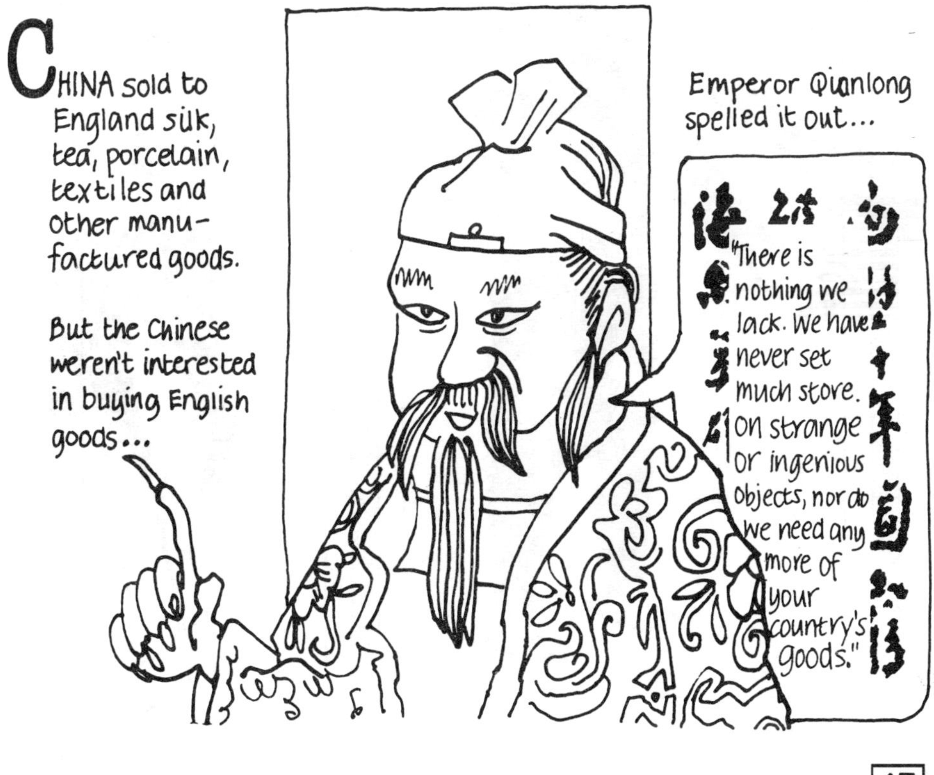
CHINA sold to England silk, tea, porcelain, textiles and other manu-factured goods.
But the Chinese weren't interested in buying English goods...
Emperor Qianlong spelled it out...
"There is nothing we lack. We have never set much store on strange or ingenious objects, nor do we need any more of your country's goods."

Dr Dinwiddie, the experimental scientist on Lord Macartney's 1793 mission, reported the Emperor Qianlong was 'heard to say when inspecting an air pump, "These things are good enough to amuse children".'

The 'foreign devil' himself; a caricature of an English sailor, circa 1840

FEUDAL China was afraid of new ideas, especially the new military hardware, that would come from outside.

Britain wasn't happy with this business set-up. Everything bought had to be paid for in hard cash!

Opium used to grow in China. But in 1729 the last of China's dynasties, the Manchus, prohibited the selling and smoking of opium. Now the British reintroduced it, by way of India, to China. The first cargo arrived in 1781.

Soon so many people became addicted that China's exports weren't enough to pay for the imported opium. The British, and then the Americans, began to amass huge fortunes.

By 1838 China was importing 40,000 chests of opium a year. A chest contained 133 pounds of opium. This was 57% of China's total imports!

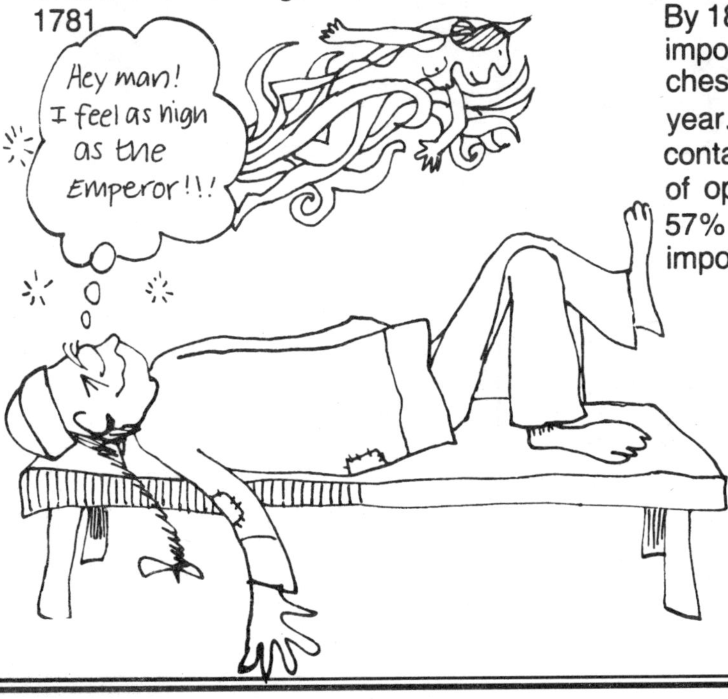

THE OPIUM WARS

It wasn't until the late 1830s that the Imperial government decided to act against the opium trade. An indignant letter was even written to Queen Victoria – which never arrived. "The great profits made by barbarians are all taken from the rightful share of China. By what right do you then use the poisonous drug to injure the Chinese people? Let us ask, where is your conscience?"

...1838—59...

Treaty of 1842

indemnification of 21 million silver dollars for the opium destroyed, and British war expenses

surrender of Hong Kong to Britain

opening of five "Treaty Ports"

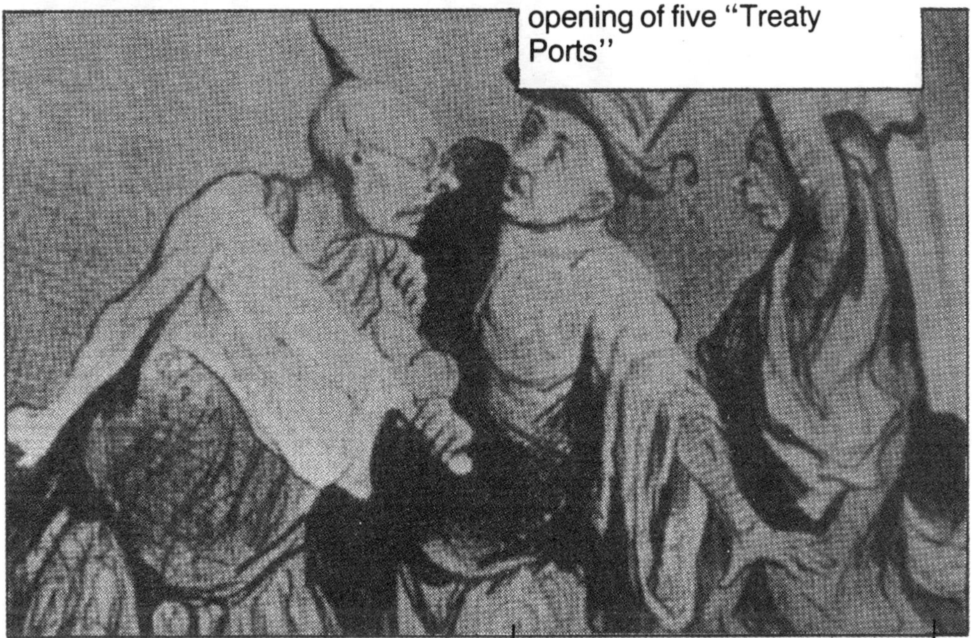

British subjects exempt from obeying Chinese law

tax exemption and only 5% custom duty on imported foreign goods

The 1844 Treaty with the U.S. was worse, because all rights given to one power had to be given to others. Including the right freely to navigate the major Chinese rivers.

LET'S not forget the saintly Christian missionaries who came to preach the doctrine of "Love thy neighbour as thyself".

The neighborhood opium dealer...

Did the missionaries stop the opium traffic? No, it increased. Did they oppose the Western gunboats? No, they travelled inland on them. Did they respect the traditional culture? No, they rode roughshod over it. With the best of motives, of course!

Two Methodist missionaries drive to work

So the Chinese people were now saddled, for another hundred years, with two enemies.

With oppressive rulers plus foreign invaders.

The crisis of Chinese society deepened.

1850

A mass revolutionary movement takes place in China.

The greatest in world history up to this time.

Peasants and artisans in southern China (next to Vietnam) rose up in arms, crossed the immense countryside and arrived at the gates of Peking, Shanghai and Tibet.

They founded a plebeian state:
The Heavenly Kingdom of Great Peace.

Taiping leader Hong Xiuquan (1814-64)

It lasted some 13 years and established a primitive sort of socialism. The Taiping rebels abolished the Manchu system of taxation, land tenure, and political control.

Peking, Shanghai, Macao and other principal cities remained in the hands of the Manchu rulers. But the Taipings scared them

half to death! And, worse yet, the foreign devils took advantage of the situation to make more trouble. In the Second Opium War (1858-60), Peking was taken by Anglo-French troops who looted and destroyed the Summer Palace.

"I never saw a demolition so complete – it does credit to the British soldier!" (Lieut. Thomas Lyster)

In the end, of course, the Manchus had to make more concessions to the foreigners.

With the new treaties a fateful bargain was sealed. Trade and religion (Western, of course) were allowed into the interior.

Foreign devils were allowed to reside in Peking – and the foreign devils suddenly became the foreign friends!

With the help of British and American mercenaries, and newly trained Chinese armies, the Manchus finally defeated their most threatening enemies – the Taiping rebels. The revenge of the government was swift and brutal. 20 million people died before the Taiping, weakened by internal squabbles, finally lost.

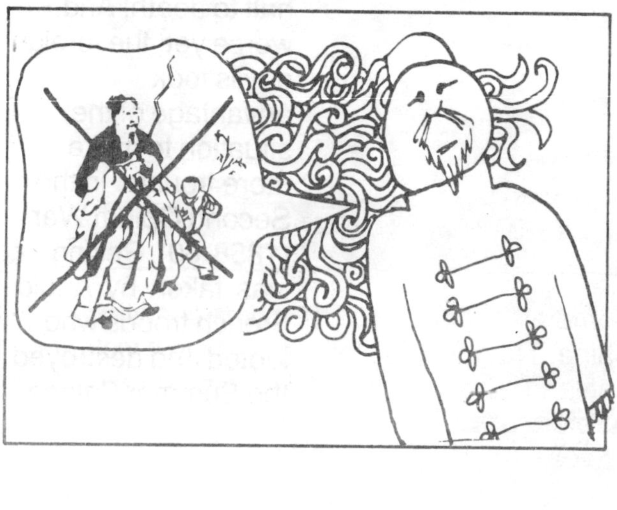

MARX published an article on the Taiping in the <u>New York Daily Tribune</u> on 14 June 1853.

"Complete isolation was the prime condition of the preservation of the old China. That isolation having come to a violent end by the medium of England, dissolution must follow as surely as that of any mummy carefully preserved in a hermetically sealed coffin whenever it is brought into contact with the open air."

K. Marx

Even though it was never really conquered, China had become a semi-colony of the great powers by the end of the 19th century. Foreigners controlled the treaty ports, the customs service, postal system, shipping, railroads and telegraph. Foreigners escaped the jurisdiction of Chinese courts. Inland rivers were patrolled by foreign gunboats. Chinese products were carried by foreign shipping in Chinese waterways. Foreign powers dominated China through their banks, war indemnities and loans.

After 1895, as foreigners began to build modern industries in China by taking advantage of cheap Chinese labour and raw materials, they also began to divide China into "Spheres of Influence".

THINGS got so bad that Chinese laborers began to go abroad in large numbers.
More like slave labor!

Coolies were shipped off to the mines and plantations of Malaysia, New Caledonia and the Western United States.

1900 The Boxer Rebellion

THE Boxers were a secret society of peasants called the YIHEQUAN or Society of the Righteous and Harmonious Fists.

The Boxers expressed a popular anti-foreign reaction, especially against Christian missionaries.

Missionaries, protected by their foreign governments, treaties and privileges, were getting hold of China bit by bit.

FED UP, the Boxers got busy: killing missionaries, attacking the foreign legations in Peking.

Real mischief-makers that lot!

Boxer cartoon of a Christian pig.

This delighted the population who hated the arrogant foreigners! The corrupt Manchu dynasty played its usual double-game. The Manchu hoped to profit from the Boxer Movement. So they declared war on the foreign powers, as if backing the popular revolt . . .

THE MANCHUS were caught between the devil (foreign, of course) and the deep blue sea (of rebellious peasants, naturally). In the end, as the foreign army approached Peking, it became clear to them where their survival lay.

Faith and Civilization are in DANGER

WITH this rallying cry, the foreign powers organized a real, old-fashioned crusade.

English, French, Austro-Hungarians, Americans, Russians, Japanese, Italians, Germans—they all got in on the act.

"Peking should be razed to the ground. Show no mercy! Take no prisoners! A thousand years ago, the Huns of King Attila made a name for themselves...thus may you impose the name of Germany in China for a thousand years."
–Kaiser William II
CIVILIZATION WAS SAFE...!

BUT... A PROPHETIC NOTE...

"Twenty millions or more of Boxers, armed, drilled, disciplined, and animated by patriotic –if mistaken – motives, will make residence in China impossible for foreigners, will take back from foreigners everything foreigners have taken from China, will pay off old grudges with interest... In fifty years' time there will be millions of Boxers in serried ranks and war's panoply at the call of the Chinese Government: there is not the slightest doubt of that!"

Sir Robert Hart, British director of China's customs system.

U.S. and European soldiers defending the diplomatic legation in Peking from Boxer attack

THE TIME HAD NOT YET COME...

Or as Mao later explained:

Execution of Boxers

"The gigantic scale of such peasant uprisings and peasant wars in Chinese history is without parallel in world history. These peasant uprisings and peasant wars alone formed the real motive force of China's historical evolution. However... the peasant revolutions invariably failed, and the peasants were utilized during or after each revolution by the landlords and the nobility as a tool for bringing about dynastic changes."

That was in 1900...

BUT the young Mao only found out when he was 15. His town had neither foreigners nor newspapers!

He had just registered at a university when new revolutionary activity broke out.

What was going on?

AN INTENSELY Nationalist group of young patriots, the majority of them students, educated abroad, organized the TONG MENGHUI, or Revolutionary Alliance. Their leader was

Dr. Sun Yatsen

SUN YATSEN had studied and lived outside China. His family was wealthy. Sun represented the ideas of Chinese living abroad, of overcoming British dominance and making China a European-style bourgeois republic.

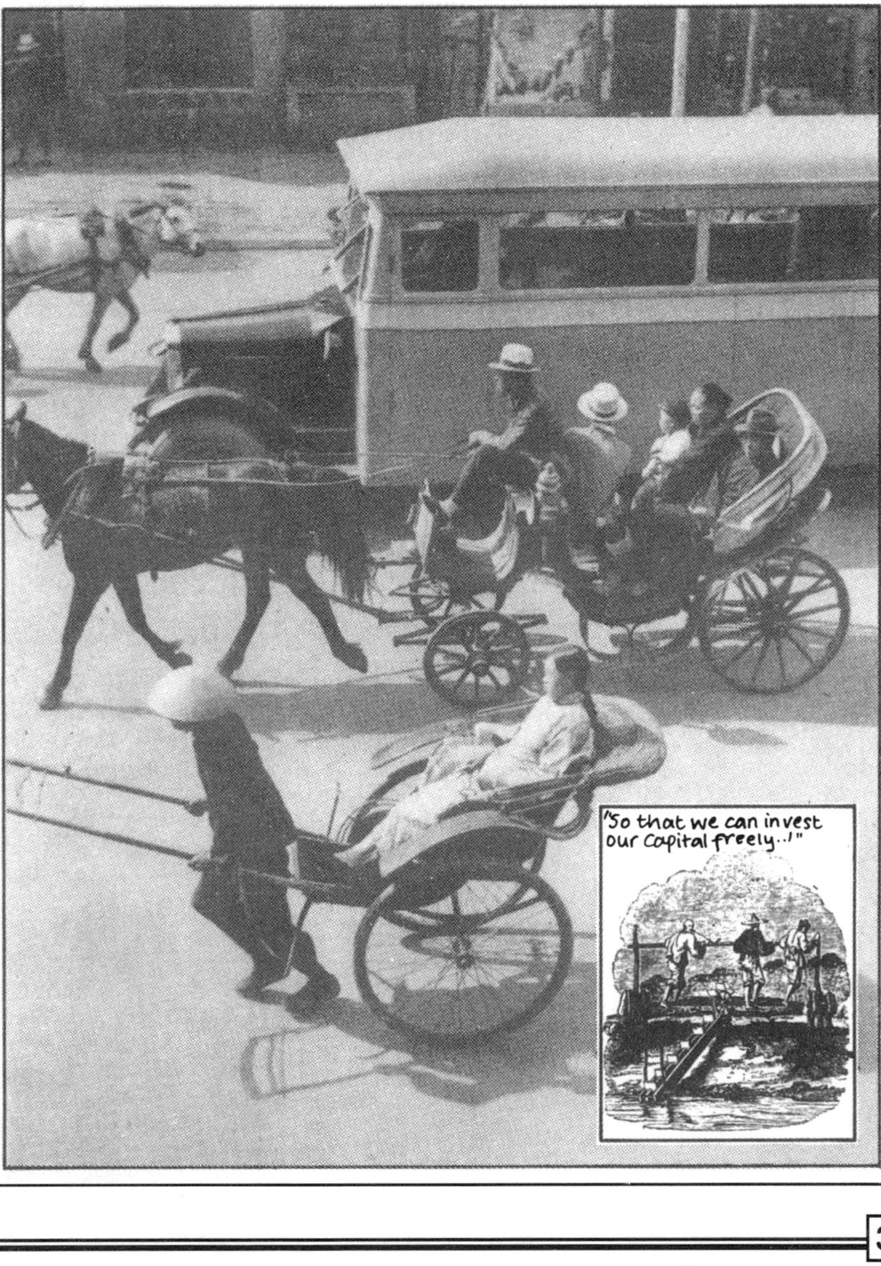

10th OCTOBER 1911

On this day began an uprising which in a year drove the Manchus from power and led to a short-lived republic in place of the age old imperial system. The Military garrison at Hankou revolted and was joined by the Imperial Navy. With the sympathies of the foreign powers, who preferred to mediate this time rather than involve themselves in a civil war, Sun's followers triumphed.

SUN YATSEN, inspirer of the revolution, returned to China after many years of exile and became Provisional President of the new republic.

The foreign powers and Chinese gentry do not like Sun's ideas...

THE WARLORDS

In the next decade, China was divided into many 'kingdoms'. At the end of the Manchu dynasty, regional armies had been created and their generals became warlords when the Manchu dynasty collapsed. They ruled their own provinces and oppressed the people in the same way, or worse, than the Manchus.

(from a letter in a Chinese newspaper)

"We must have soldiers, people say, so that the country will be strong. We must have armies to protect ourselves from foreigners. And the armies are continually recruiting men. And the people become poorer and poorer! Our old Lao Tse said it so well: where an army has passed, nothing grows but brambles. This is the case with us, where armies pass through again and again. Our situation has become intolerable... Let us not mince words, soldiers and bandits are two names for the same thing."

Wu Peifu (1874-1939)

Zang Zuolin (1873-1928)

Feng Yuxiang (1882-1948)

THE KUOMINTANG

The Kuomintang, or the National People's Party, was founded in 1912.

Incidentally, 'TANG' means 'party'.

THE KUOMINTANG, the majority party in the new parliament, was a union of radical republicans and groups influenced by the 1905 Russian Revolution.

Conflicts soon developed between the Kuomintang and the military cliques.

Sun Yatsen, as leader of the Kuomintang, set up a regime in Canton. It was as weak as the official, western-recognized government in Peking. Neither could control the warlords.

The Kuomintang circa 1912

THE FIRST WORLD

DURING much of this war, China remained neutral, but was forced to declare war on Germany on 14th August 1917.

WAR—1914-18

JAPAN was on the Allied side. This was a good excuse for the Japanese to invade north China, defeat the small German army stationed there, and take over the German possessions.

SO BEGAN Japan's attempt to turn China into a Japanese colony.

EUROPEANS were busy with the slaughter at home. And China was so divided itself that nobody could do much to stop the Japanese.

4th MAY 1919

Having entered the war on the Allied side, the Chinese fully expected victory to mean the return of Germany's Chinese possessions. When the news reached China that the Versailles Conference had simply transferred Germany's rights and privileges in Shandong to Japan, many Chinese felt betrayed. On May 4, 1919, students organized protest demonstrations which soon swept the nation. Even a rail strike – the first recorded in Chinese history occurred.

For the first time, both intellectuals and workers linked foreign imperialism with domestic reaction in a single slogan: "Externally preserve our sovereignty and internally eliminate the traitors!"

May Fourth also represented the beginning of a great revolt of intellectuals against the oppressive weight of the Confucian cultural tradition. Lu Hsun, the outstanding intellectual iconoclast of this period, urged Chinese writers to break with the classical tradition and write in the vernacular. In a famous story, THE DIARY OF A MADMAN, he savagely parodied the old Confucian society as cannibalistic: "I recollect, in ancient times, people often ate human beings, but I am rather hazy about it. I tried to look this up, but my history (the Confucian canon) has no chronology, and scrawled over each page are the words: 'Virtue and Morality.'

In any case, I could not sleep, so I read half the night, until I began to see words between the lines, the whole book being filled with the two words, 'Eat People.'"

Lu Hsun

Chou Enlai was a student organizer in Tianjin

"The Salvos of the October Revolution brought us Marxism-Leninism." Mao

MANY already knew that the Russian revolution of 1917 had finished-off the Tsar and was defending itself successfully against the expeditionary troops of Britain, France, Japan and the United States.

Li Dazhao, a lecturer at Peking University, and later, a founder of the Chinese Communist Party was one of the first to respond to the news.

"We laboring, impoverished people were suffering under two types of oppression when suddenly the October Revolution called for the 'overthrow of world capitalism' and the 'overthrow of world imperialism'! The October Revolution has the very greatest historical significance."

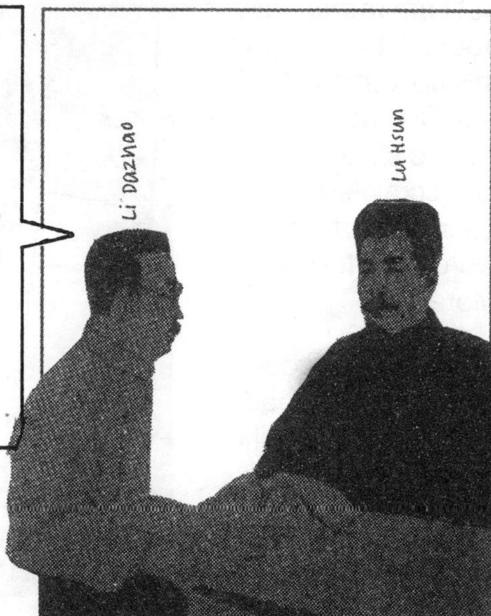

WHAT ABOUT MAO?

For 6 months, in 1911, young Mao served in the new republican army. This was a turbulent time. But between 1911 and 1918 Mao studied at Changsha, provincial capital of Hunan, until he graduated as a teacher from the Normal School there.

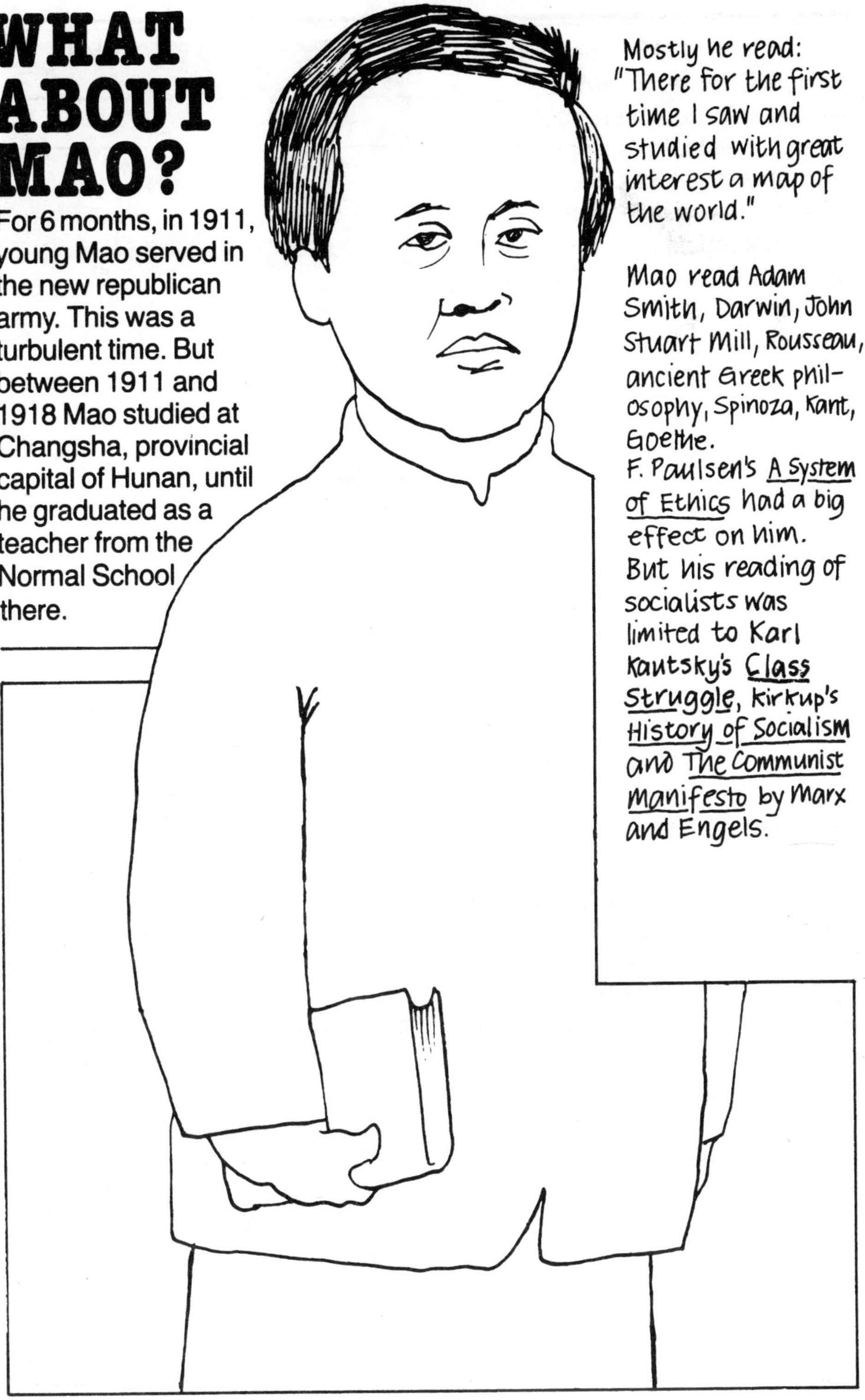

In Changsha, 1918, Mao founded the New Citizens Society, a discussion group of energetic young activists. "We slept in the open when frost was already falling and even in November swam in the cold rivers. All this went on under the title of 'body training'."

"Exercise should be savage and rude," Mao wrote at this time. "To be able to leap on horseback and to shoot at the same time; to go from battle to battle; to shake the mountains by one's cries, and the colours of the sky by one's roars of anger... all this is savage and rude and has nothing to do with delicacy."

Even then, what separated Mao from so many others was his faith in the power of the masses. "Our Chinese people possess great intrinsic energy. The more profound the oppression, the greater the resistance; that which has accumulated for a long time will surely burst forth quickly... Our golden age, our age of brilliance and splendour, lies ahead!"

Li Dazhao found Mao a menial job in the library at Peking University.

That was in 1918.

Mao read Tolstoy, Kropotkin and Bakunin, and for a few months considered himself an anarchist. "My own living conditions in Peking were quite miserable, and in contrast, the beauty of the old capital was a vivid and living compensation. I stayed in a place called San Yenching (Three Eyes Well), in a little room which held seven other people. When we were all packed fast on the *kang* (a large bed made of earth heated from underneath) there was scarcely enough room for any of us to breathe. I used to warn people on either side of me when I wanted to turn over. But in the parks and the old palace grounds I saw the early northern spring, I saw the white plum blossoms while the ice still held solid over Pei Hai . . ."

IN PEKING, Mao fell in love with Yang Kaihui, daughter of a professor of philosophy. They married in 1921 and had two sons.

Contrary to Chinese custom, Mao and Yang married for love.

(Their romance has even been told in a popular Chinese comic book. See below.)

Will our hero find True Love?..

MAO's father had already arranged one marriage for him when he was 13— with a girl six years older.

This was by no means uncommon.

The girl would work for the Mao household before the marriage was consummated, which meant the Maos acquired a servant as well as a bride (some system eh?)

Mao refused to have anything to do with this marriage, ran away from home and would not return until his father gave up the plan.

....Read on...

Oh! By the way, Yang Kaihui isn't the Mrs Mao of "Gang of Four" fame. She was his first wife who, as you'll read later, came to a tragic end in 1930.

LATER, when Mao was a student at Changsha, his first published articles were about the unhappy position of women in traditional China.

He heard of the suicide of a young girl who had slit her throat rather than go through with her arranged marriage.

"The circumstances in which Miss Chao found herself were the following: (1) Chinese society; (2) the Chao family of Nanyang Street in Changsha; (3) the Wu family of Kantzuyuan Street in Changsha, the family of the husband she did not want. These three factors constituted three iron nets, composing a kind of triangular

cage. Once caught in these three nets, it was in vain that she sought life in every way possible."

From early on, Mao emphasized how much worse off women were than men in feudal China because they were dominated by their husbands <u>and</u> parents-in-law.

This was in accordance with the Confucian ethical system.

MAO'S concern for the position of women continued throughout his life.

The first law passed in the People's Republic, after Liberation, was the Land Law which gave women equal rights to hold land.

This was followed by the Marriage Law which protected girls against arranged marriages and provided for divorce.

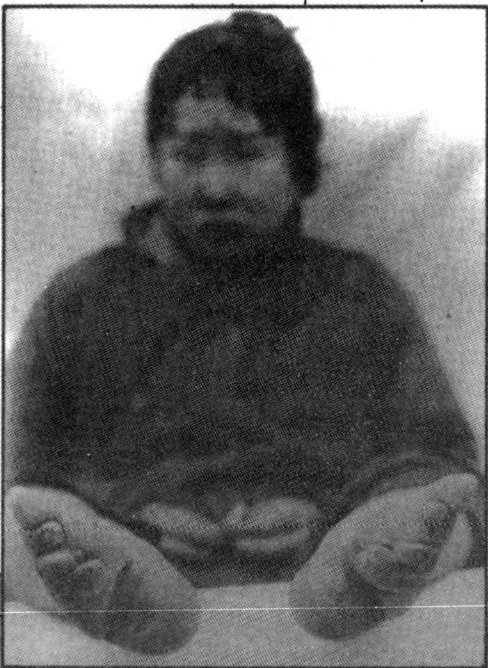

The old custom of foot-binding – to produce small 'aristocratic' feet!

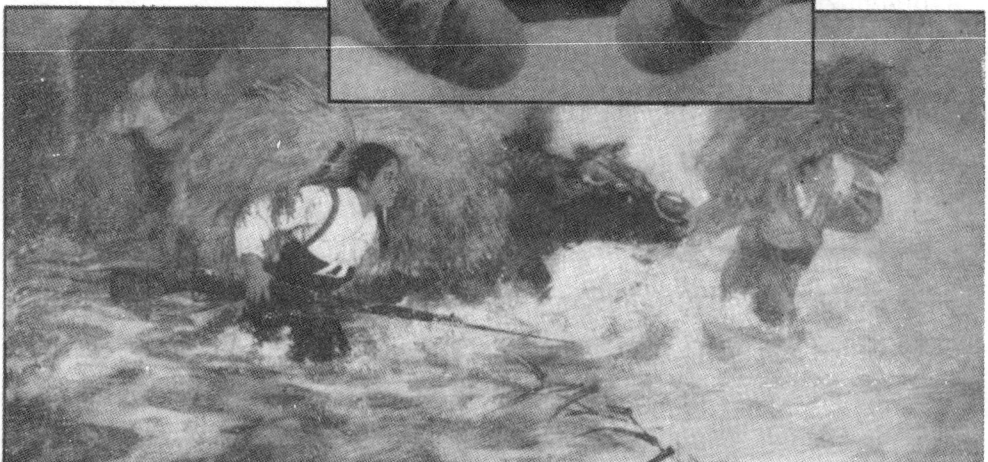

THE SUMMER OF 1921

TWO PEKING University lecturers, Chen Duxiu and Li Dazhao, were the main organizers.

THEY wrote to every leftist organization in China. But there were only 12 delegates at the first Congress of the C.C.P.

Fleeing from the police, the delegates held their congress on a damn sampan!

MAO and his comrades faced some tough going. To organize peasants and workers and bring them into the Communist Party – was not easy.

Still, the results were encouraging. Strikes in the major cities among miners, railway-workers, seamen, fishermen and artisans.

Unions arose, directed by Communists.

Did the Soviet Union help?

THE CHINESE C.P. in the early 1920s was small and weak.

Salvation for China seemed to lie with the bigger, influential Kuomintang.

SOVIET agents A.A. Joffe and Henricus Sneevliet negotiated with Sun Yatsen. The USSR promised to support the Kuomintang and train Sun's armies.

Sneevliet (alias Maring / 1883 - 1942) played an important role in persuading the Chinese Communists to enter into an alliance with the Kuomintang and to accept a bourgeois-led struggle for national liberation.

But he became deeply disillusioned by the capitalist powers, and turned more and more towards Russia. "If we wish our revolution to succeed, we must learn the methods of organization and training of the Russians; then there can be hope of success."

The Chinese Communists took part in Sun's Kuomintang government at Canton. A military academy was founded there and left under a young officer, Chiang Kaishek.

Its political commissar was another young man, Chou Enlai.

Chou Enlai

In 1925 the pro-Japanese government in Peking felt obliged to approach Sun Yatsen and propose a conference on the theme: "the peaceful unification of the country". Sun, in turn proposed the democratic election of a National Assembly to rule China without foreign intervention.

But Sun died suddenly of cancer shortly after his arrival in Peking.

The Kuomintang was left in the hands of...

Chiang Kaishek

Meanwhile the Kuomintang prepared for war against the powerful warlords of the north, Zhang Zuolin, Wu Peifu, Feng Yuxiang.

It wasn't General Chiang Kaishek, but the fighting spirit of the peasants and workers which demolished the resistance of the warlords.

In 1924 the Communist Party had only 500 members. But with the rise of a militant working class movement, the Party gained over 58,000 members by the beginning of 1927.

In the rural areas

millions of peasants were flocking to peasant associations and rising against the landlords.

Chiang Kaishek's army rode to victory on the crest of this mass upheaval.

However, the leaders of the KMT began to fear social revolution.

What about Mao?

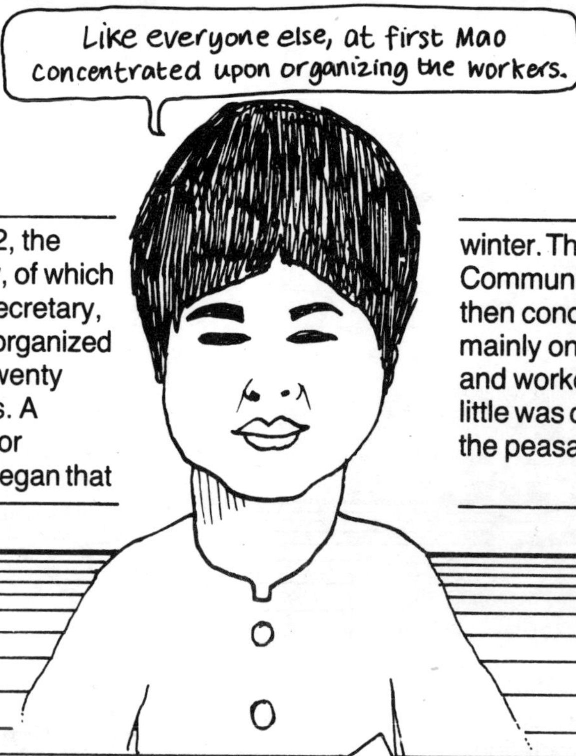

"In May, 1922, the Hunan Party, of which I was then secretary, had already organized more than twenty trade unions. A vigorous labor movement began that winter. The work of the Communist Party was then concentrated mainly on students and workers and very little was done among the peasants."

The Russians had a Magic Formula:

The Industrial Proletariat is the Vanguard of the Revolution!

But Mao argued that China was a country of peasants.

Revolution must come from the countryside, not from the cities, Canton, Shanghai or Peking.

But Mao's ideas don't count in the Chinese Communist Party...

THE DISAGREEMENT WAS

"The peasants are widely scattered, therefore, it is not easy to organize them into an effective force. Their cultural standards being low and needs being simple, their outlook is therefore conservative. China

being a big country, making it easy for them to migrate, they tend to shy away from difficulty and become complacent. These are the three factors preventing them from participating in the revolution."

Chen Duxiu, leader of the Communist Party

"In a short time . . . several million peasants will rise like a mighty storm, like a hurricane, a force so swift and violent that no power, however great, will be able to hold it back. They will smash all the trammels that bind them and rush forward along the

FUNDAMENTAL

road to liberation. They will sweep all the imperialists, warlords, corrupt officials, local tyrants and evil gentry into their graves. Every revolutionary party and every revolutionry comrade will be put to the test, to be accepted or rejected as they decide. There are three alternatives. To march at their head and lead them? To trail behind them, gesticulating and criticizing? Or to stand in their way and oppose them? Every Chinese is free to choose, but events will force you to make the choice quickly."

Mao Tsetung: 1927.

AND WHAT ABOUT STALIN THEN?

Did he know who the enemies of the Chinese Communists were?

STALIN was clear in his directives to the Chinese C.P.:

"It would be the greatest mistake for the Chinese Communists to leave the Kuomintang."

Don't upset the alliance! Curb peasant excesses! Don't seize the land of Chiang's associates!

A week before Chiang turned on the Communists, Stalin said;

"We are told that Chiang Kaishek is making ready to turn against us again. I know that he is playing a cunning game with us, but it is He that will be crushed. We shall squeeze him like a lemon and then be rid of him."

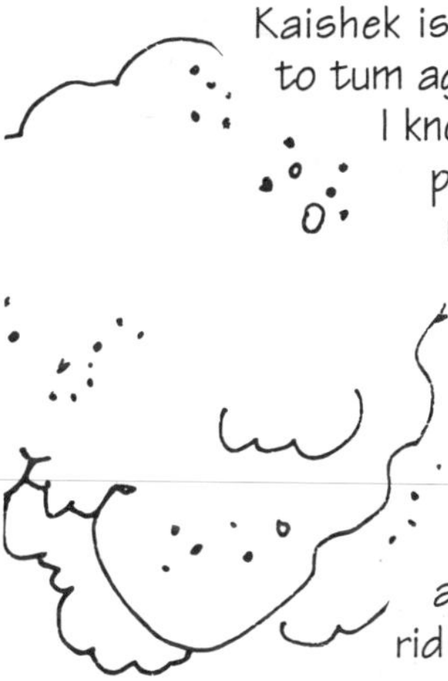

The Party remains confused—and the rebellious workers and peasants are left defenseless and largely leaderless in the face of the forces of counter-revolution preparing to suppress them.

Soviet advisers with Sun Yatsen

Soviet Ambassador Chicherin in Mongol dress

BUT WHAT ABOUT CHIANG KAISHEK?

The Chinese Communists, Chou Enlai and his comrades, organize a workers' insurrection against the military rulers in Shanghai.

Their general strike goes well.

The workers are about to seize power, when...

CHIANG Kaishek had diverted his Army towards Shanghai.

The Communist-led workers were ready to welcome the Kuomintang 'revolutionary' army.

But General Chiang Kaishek negotiated secretly with the bankers who promised him big money from the Western powers if he co-operated.

ANDRE Malraux's famous novel, <u>Man's Fate</u>, describes what happened on 12th April 1927.

GENERAL Chiang Kaishek's troops turned against the Shanghai workers. In a bloody massacre almost all the members of the Communist Party were killed. Chou Enlai escaped.

AFTER that Chinese St. Bartholomew's Eve, Chiang Kaishek became the favourite leader of the United States.

The Free World now had its hero...

(its long-lasting hero too, as this later photo shows)

SIMILAR massacres occurred in other cities under Kuomintang rule.

But the Communists still didn't break with the traitor Chiang!

In a few weeks, the Chinese Communist Party lost 15,000 members, and in the white terror that followed, hundreds of thousands of Chinese workers and peasants were slaughtered.
The labour movement, decimated, went underground, not to reemerge until 1949.

Mao didn't die, but his ideas of peasant revolt and his opposition to the absurd alliance with the KMT (Kuomintang) left him in disagreement with the Communist Party leaders.

COUNTER-ATTACK...

& DEFEAT

THE Chinese Communists now wanted to give the KMT a taste of its own medicine.

IN JULY 1927, after the defeat in Shanghai, the party organised an uprising in Nanking. It failed. The Chinese C.P. was outlawed and Mao was declared "a Red Bandit!"

Mao organized the peasant unions and Hanyang miners into the First Workers' and Peasants' Revolutionary Army.

The C.P. still hadn't given up! It ordered Mao's army to attack the cities. In September, 1927 Mao participated in the Autumn Harvest uprisings in Hunan and Kiangsi provinces.

"I was captured by some *mintuan* (militia) working with the Kuomintang. The Kuomintang terror was then at its height and hundreds of suspected Reds were being shot.

I was ordered to be taken to the *mintuan* headquarters, where I was to be killed. Borrowing several tens of dollars from a comrade, however, I attempted to bribe the escort to free me. The ordinary soldiers were mercenaries, with no special interest in seeing me killed, and so they agreed to release me, but the subaltern in charge refused to permit it. I therefore decided to attempt to escape, but had no opportunity to do so until I was within about 200 yards of the *mintuan* headquarters. At that point I broke loose and ran into the fields."

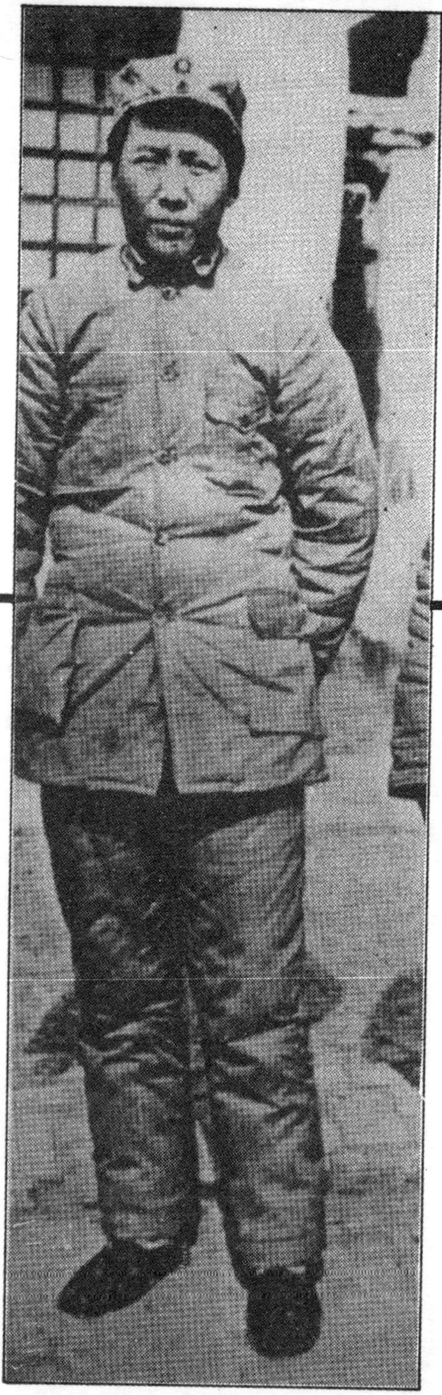

CHIANG Kaishek consolidated his rule with the support of foreign powers.

Mao and other surviving, obstinate communists started something new for them:

The Guerrilla War...

HARDLY a thousand men, armed with only 200 rifles, now settled in the mountains of Jingangshan, strategically placed at the frontiers of three provinces.

In May, 1928, an unexpected ally turned up.

Zhu De, ex-policeman, ex-opium addict, ex-owner of many concubines!

Hold on! Zhu De has changed. For years he's been a serious communist. He is a great fighter, and he brings with him almost 2,000 men!

Others soon arrived. Eight thousand peasants joined the new-born Red Army!
Now they were too many, crowded, without arms, food or clothing. Best look for another hideaway...!

'NOTHING grows in these mountains. No one here, either peasants or townsfolk. We can't continue the struggle here!'
So, on tiptoe, Mao and half the army headed towards Juichin in Kiangsi, another mountain stronghold.
A real raggedy-pants army...!

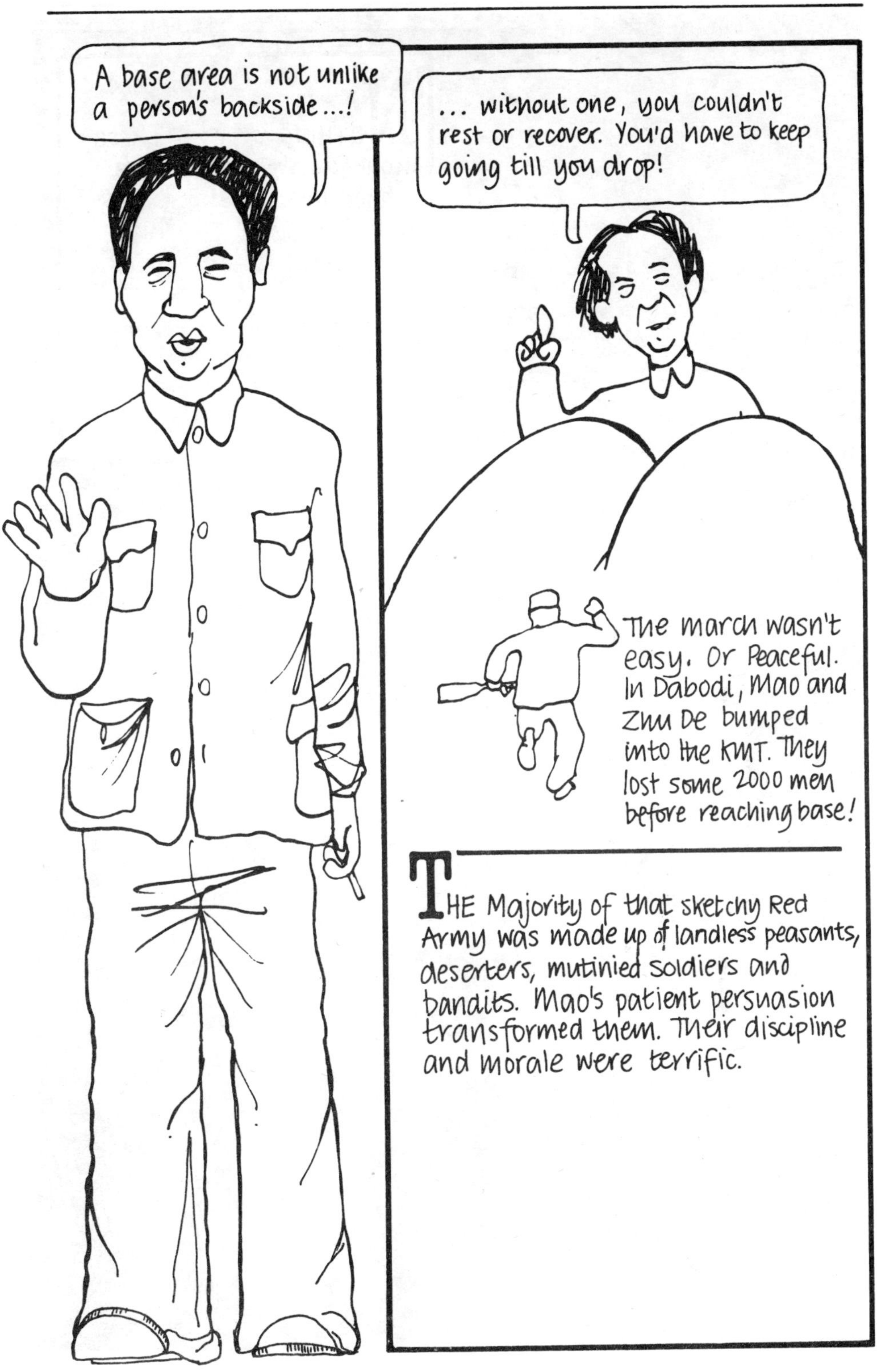
A base area is not unlike a person's backside...!
... without one, you couldn't rest or recover. You'd have to keep going till you drop!
The march wasn't easy. Or Peaceful. In Dabodi, Mao and Zhu De bumped into the KMT. They lost some 2000 men before reaching base!
THE Majority of that sketchy Red Army was made up of landless peasants, deserters, mutinied soldiers and bandits. Mao's patient persuasion transformed them. Their discipline and morale were terrific.

Mao in 1933

Mao's rules for survival-

1 Obey orders in all your actions

2 Do not take a single needle or a piece of thread from the masses.

3 Turn in everything captured.

And the following
NORMS OF CONDUCT

- Speak politely.
- Pay fairly for what you buy.
- Return everything you borrow.
- Pay for anything you damage.
- Do not hit or swear at people.
- Do not damage crops.
- Do not take liberties with women.
- Do not ill-treat captives.

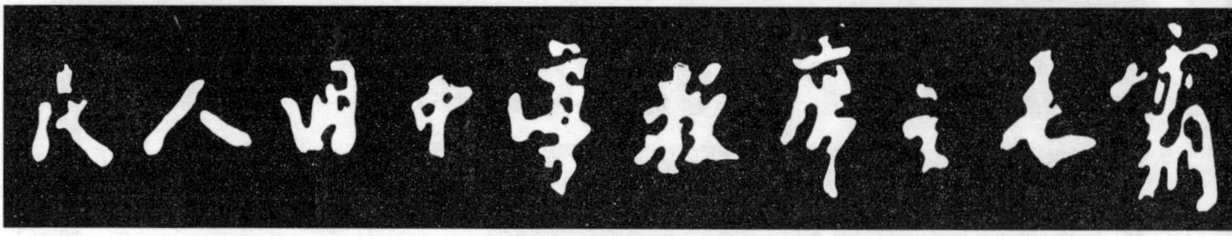

TILL then, people were used to armies of looters, murderers, rapists and arsonists. Mao's Red Army was a nice surprise!

No wonder it made allies.

IN CHINA a new kind of army was born: an army *of* the people to defend the people.

深挖洞廣積粮不称

GUERRILLA tactics are summed up by Mao:

When the enemy advances, we retreat.

When the enemy camps, we harass.

When the enemy tires, we attack.

Mao is the greatest tactician of guerrilla warfare.

He teaches the 5 requirements for victory:

1 Support from the masses
2 Party organization
3 Strong guerrilla army
4 Favourable region for military moves
5 Economic self-sufficiency

But how could such a ragtag peasant army hope to seize power? How could they even claim to be communists?

During the next decade, Mao figured this out. First he asked himself: What kind of a country is China anyway? The answer: a "semi-colonial, semi-feudal nation."

What did he mean by this:

"China's political and economic development is uneven – a weak capitalist economy coexists with a preponderant semi-feudal economy; a few modern industrial and commercial cities coexist with a vast stagnant countryside; several million industrial workers coexist with several hundred millions of peasants and handicraftsmen labouring under the old system; big warlords controlling the central government coexist with small warlords controlling the provinces; two kinds of reactionary armies, the so-called Central Army under Chiang Kaishek and 'miscellaneous troops' under the warlords in the provinces, exist side by side; a few railways, steamship lines and motor roads exist side by side with a vast number of wheelbarrow paths and foot-paths many of which are difficult to negotiate even on foot."

BUT how could China's semi-colonial, semi-feudal nature assist Mao when it came to the question of seizing power?

Disunity and rivalry among the imperialist powers makes for disunity among the ruling groups in China.

The forces of imperialism can successfully control the cities, but not the impoverished rural hinterland.

National capitalism is less able to fully develop in China so the bourgeoisie are unable to make their own revolution.

Such disarray and weakness leaves space for the mobilization of the peasants, the creation of a red army, and the setting up of base areas in remote areas of the countryside!

CHIANG KAISHEK in 1930 decided to wipe out Mao's 'Red Bandits' and launched 5 "Extermination Campaigns".

Chiang's forces were superior by 10 to 1. But the KMT troops were defeated in 4 straight campaigns!

They simply could not grasp Mao's strategy of mobility and so the 'ragged bandits' of the Red Army were able to relieve them of a great quantity of arms!

IN JULY 1930, Yang Kaihui was captured and killed by the KMT. Not only did they murder Mao's young wife, but also his younger sister.

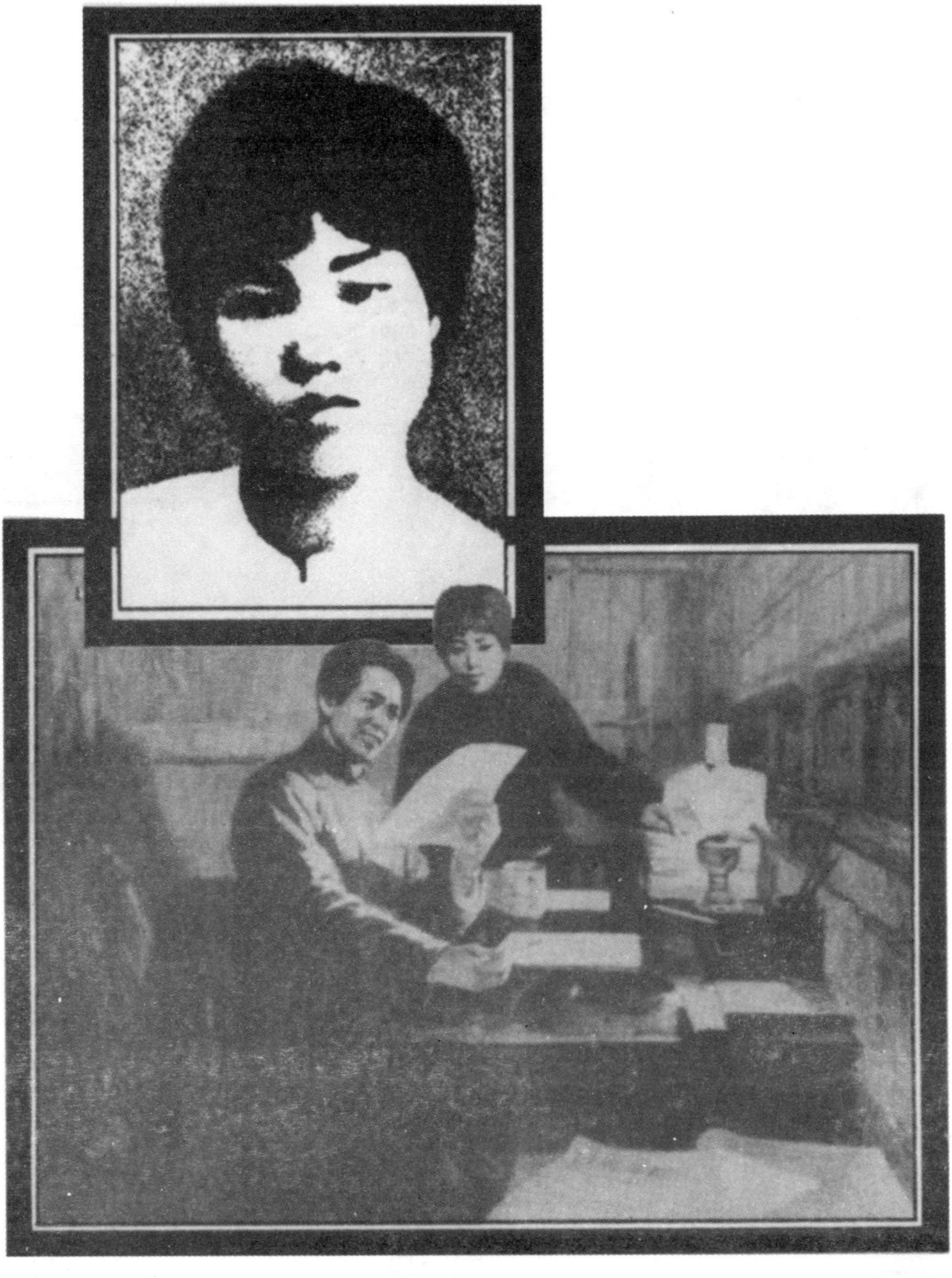

CHIANG'S campaign lasted 4 years.

Four complete disasters for him!

He was also being pressured by the Japanese who were threatening to invade China from the North.

The Reds!

CHIANG decided to minimize the Japanese threat.

Under his personal command, Chiang led a 900,000-man army, formations of 300 bombers, plus a German advisor, General Von Seeckt, against Mao.

CHIANG now changed his tactics. *(It was about time after 4 defeats!!)*

He adopted a 'scorched earth' policy. His army razed everything to the ground wherever it passed.

By August, 1934, The Communist forces, already reduced to 100,000 men, found themselves encircled.
The pincers were about to close.
And they did close...
ONCE the circle had closed, Mao called a conference to decide what to do.
世上无难事
只要肯登攀
After long, intense discussions a decision was reached...

Let's go...

THE FORCES were regrouped in one place. At night. In the rain. With their weapons and a few belongings on their backs, about 100,000 men, 35 women and a few children crossed enemy lines.

So began...

THE LONG MARCH

MAYBE WE SHOULD SAY:

THE GREAT

MARCH

THE Red Army began its retreat on 16th October 1934.

CHIANG Kaishek was on their heels. Constantly pursued, ambushed, bombed, decimated by hunger and disease: the Red Army had just one objective:

TO SURVIVE!

The illustrations on this and the next few pages are from a folio produced by an artist on the March.

AN OLD iron bridge over the Tatu River had most of its wooden planks removed by KMT troops on the other side. Some two dozen volunteers began to cross over, dangling from the chains, swinging across link by link.

Many were picked off by KMT sniping and fell into the roaring gorge some 300 feet

elow. But a few managed to each the other side and lthough weary and greatly utnumbered, overwhelmed the nemy troops. At last, the vay north was clear.

In the gorges of this remote Tatu river the last of the Taiping rebels had been destroyed by the Manchu armies.

The Routes of the Long March

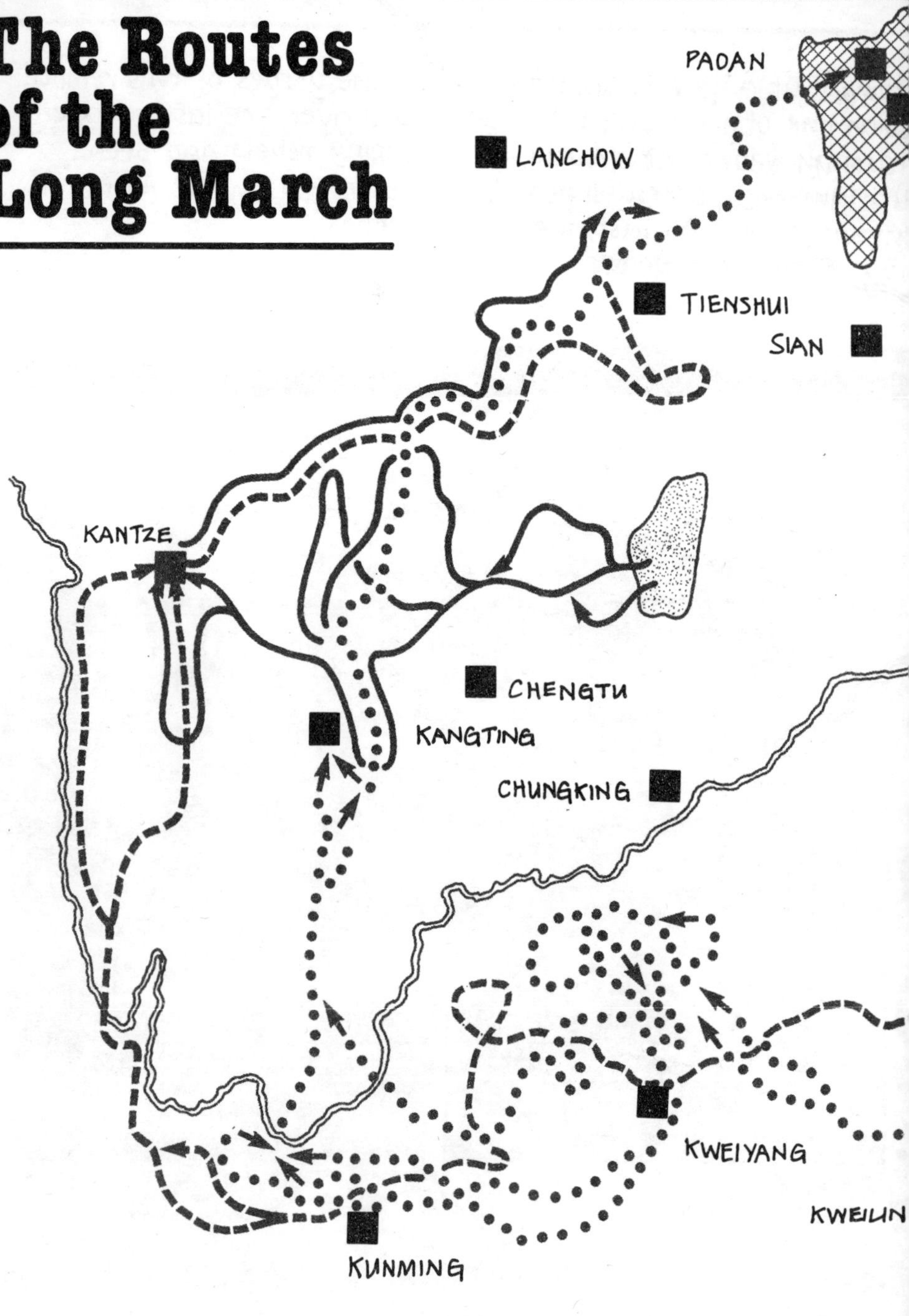

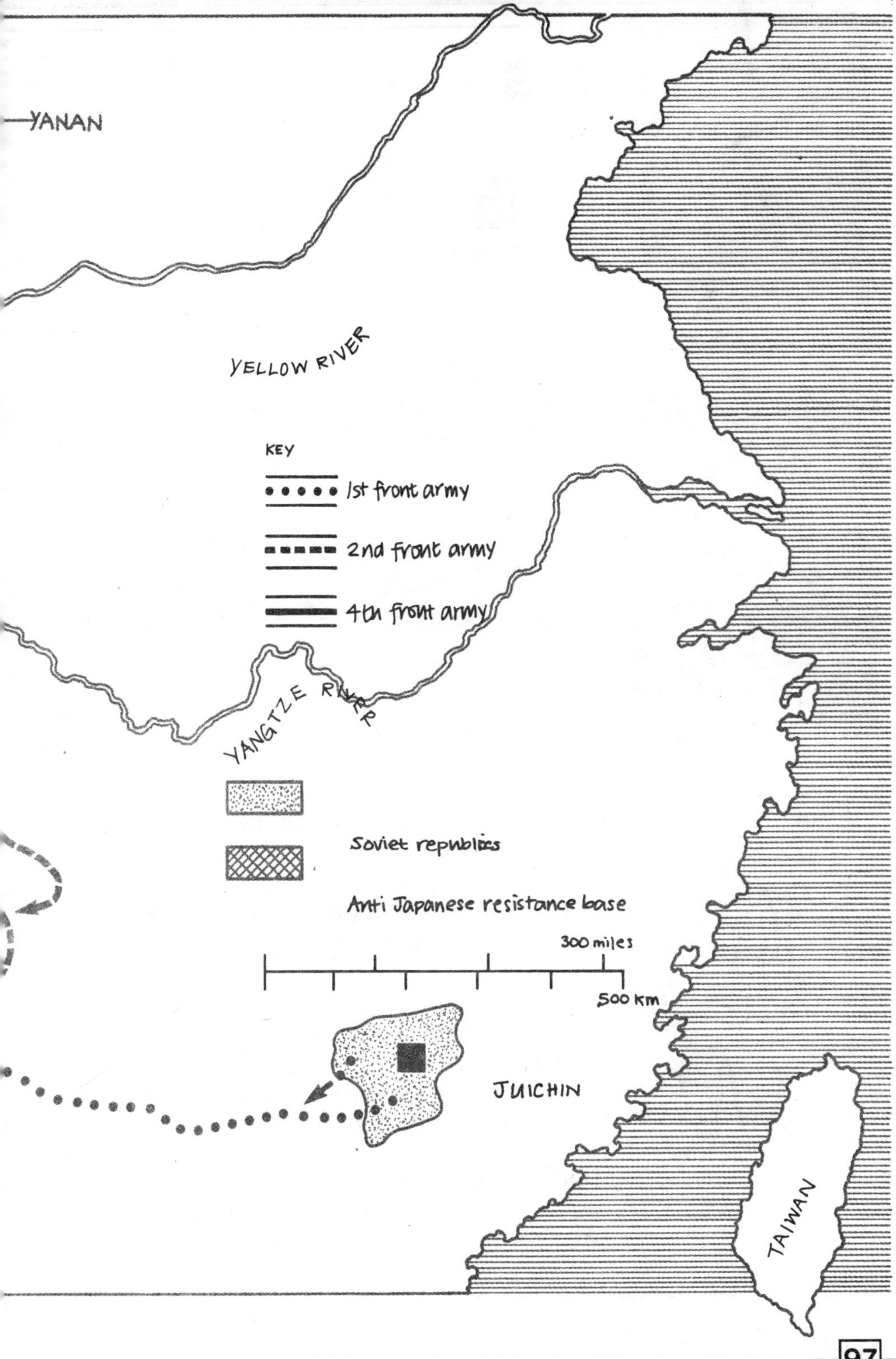
YANAN
YELLOW RIVER
KEY
1st front army
2nd front army
4th front army
YANGTZE RIVER
Soviet republics
Anti Japanese resistance base
300 miles
500 km
JUICHIN
TAIWAN

THEY covered six thousand miles (yes, that's right, 6000!).

They fought the KMT forces—and the Warlords whose regions they crossed.

They climbed 18 mountain chains, forded 24 rivers, traversed deserts and swamps.

Almost all the women died and the children were left along the way. But Mao's pregnant second wife, Ho Tzuchen, got through the whole march with him.

During that dreadful march some 80,000 men died. Less than one-fifth of the Red Army finally reached Yenan.

WELL, it broke the KMT encirclement...

And at Yenan (if you don't mind, we'll use YANAN, the Pinyin system of spelling), after 368 days on the march, a firm base was established – and the beginnings of a socialist republic.

But Mao said it was a defeat...

"Except for the Shensi-Kansu border areas, all revolutionary bases were lost, the Red Army reduced from 300,000 to a few tens of thousands, the membership of the Chinese Communist Party was reduced from 300,000 to a few tens of thousands, and the Party organizations in Kuomintang areas were almost entirely wiped out. In short, we received an extremely great historical punishment."

But Mao also said it was a great victory!

"We answer that the Long March is the first of its kind in the annals of history, that it is a manifesto, a propaganda force, a seeding machine . . . It has proclaimed to the world that the Red Army is an army of heroes, while the imperialists and their running dogs, Chiang Kai-shek and his like, are impotent. It has proclaimed their utter failure to encircle, pursue, obstruct and intercept us . . . It has announced to some 200 million people in eleven provinces that the road of the Red Army is their only road to liberation."

CHIANG Kaishek wanted to get rid of the Reds. Mao wanted to get rid of Chiang. And the Japanese...

What about Japan?

IMPERIAL Japan was about to start the formal invasion of China.

Chiang was indifferent—too busy with Mao.

Mao, instead, thought the main enemy was Japan, and he was even willing to unite with Chiang to combat Japan.

Even the Russians agreed, and said as much:

THE SIAN INCIDENT

DECEMBER 12th, 1936, Chiang Kaishek was kidnapped by two former warlords and allies of Chiang's, Zhang Xueliang and Yang Hucheng.
Mao was consulted.

Chiang was being offered up for execution!

CHIANG was accused of pro-Japanese treason. He might have been tried and executed. But Stalin himself wanted Chiang's life spared!

FACED WITH death, Chiang called off his next "suppression campaign" against the communists.

Chou Enlai negotiated (though Chiang had put a price of $80,000 on his head!). Chiang agreed to fight Japan with Mao!

Chiang Kaishek

Zhang Xueliang

CAN Chiang be trusted?

But once again, alliance with the Koumintang was accepted.

Meanwhile...

Ah! another world war is about to explode!

In July 1937 Japan invaded China

Chiang Kaishek briefly fought the Japanese. In the first year of the war, his armies were driven out of the cities and deep inland. From then until 1945 the KMT undertook no major initiatives against the Japanese.

Chou Enlai said it: "The first day of the anti-Japanese war will mean the beginning of the end for Chiang Kaishek." Why? Because Chiang had lost his base in the coastal cities. He did not dare to mobilize the peasants whom he feared would turn against him.

WHILE Chiang Kaishek played politics with the allies, the real fighting against Japan was done by the Communists.

Incredibly, U.S. and Soviet help was not for Mao—but for that traitor, Chiang, because he was the 'head' of the Chinese government. (If you can find any sense in that—let me know!)

THE YANAN EXPERIENCE (1937-1949)

"It was not until the period of the resistance to Japan that we formulated a general line for the Party and a complete set of concrete policies which were appropriate to the actual situation. By this time we had been making revolution for more than twenty years. For so many years previously we were working very much in the dark. If anyone were to claim that any comrade, for example any member of the Central Committee, or I myself, completely understood the laws of the Chinese revolution right from the beginning, then that comrade would be talking through his hat. He should definitely not be believed. It was not like that at all. In the past, and especially at the beginning, all our energies were directed toward revolution, but as for how to make revolution, what we wanted to change, which should come first and which later, and which should wait until the next stage — for a fairly long time none of these questions were properly understood, or we could say they were not thoroughly understood."

Mao.

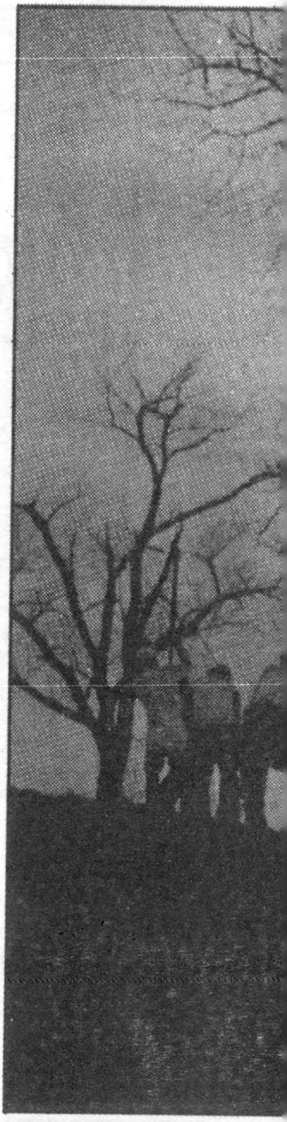

In fact, the bulk of Mao's writings later canonized as the "thoughts of Mao Tsetung" were composed in the Yanan period.

WHAT ABOUT MAO'S OWN MARXISM?

"Seventeen and eighteen-year-old babies are taught to nibble on Das Kapital and Anti-Duhring . . . Their inclination is to regard what they have learned from their teachers as never changing dogma."

MAO WANTED TO THROW ABSTRACT MARXISM OUT OF THE WINDOW

"Those who regard Marxism-Leninism as religious dogma show . . . blind ignorance. We must tell them openly, 'Your dogma is of no use,' or to use an impolite phrase, 'Your dogma is less useful than excrement.' We see that dog excrement can fertilize the fields, and man's can feed the dog. And dogmas? They can't fertilize the fields, nor can they feed the dog. Of what use are they?"

THEN WHAT WAS 'ABSTRACT MARXISM'?

"If a Chinese Communist who is a part of the great Chinese people, bound to his people by his flesh and blood, talks of Marxism apart from Chinese peculiarities, this Marxism is merely an empty abstraction . . . The Sinification of Marxism . . . becomes a problem that must be understood and solved by the whole Party without delay."

IT WAS SOVIET MARXISM APPLIED TO CHINA...

In the liberated base area of Yanan in one of the poorest, most desolate regions of North China, Mao began to put Chinese Marxism into practice. The communists organized themselves both militarily and economically, with the principal task still remaining the defeat of Japan.

They reduced land rent and fixed low interest rates; but, at the same time, encouraged cooperative work in agriculture and industry. They organized schools, universities, technological training institutes and art schools. Their system of mass organization and participation in government was called "Democratic Centralism". It was based on the principle of "from the people to the people", which, in practice, meant that the masses must be consulted, decisions made on the basis of such consultation, and these decisions explained to the masses.

This involved a new, egalitarian vision in China!

What did Mao say fuels the whole process of revolution? The Masses! Formerly they lived at the margin of existence, their livelihood prey to natural disasters, their very existence under the control of all-powerful landlords. Mao knew that if they were offered a way out, they would take it; and Mao was able to show them that this way out was through a whole range of cooperative methods. BUT FIRST, they had to be allowed to come to center stage, to experience their collective power. In Yanan, the communists organized a new and startling form of collective drama.

"What was it that won over most villages to us? The Speak Bitterness sessions. We organized these in every village."
– Mao

For the first time in their lives, peasants were encouraged to stand up to their oppressors — the landlords. Jack Belden, an American journalist, provided a moving description of the process: "Scarface, Crooked Head, Lop Ear — the number of these nameless creatures was legion in the land. For such a man to stand up and speak before his fellow-villagers, both rich and poor, constituted by its very nature a revolutionary break with the past. In the same moment that he burst through the walls of silence that had enveloped him all his life, the peasant also tore asunder the chains that had bound him to feudalism. Awkwardly, at first the words crawled from his throat, but once the first word passed his lips, there came gushing forth, not only an unarrestable torrent of speech, but the peasant's soul."

Again Belden: "In the women of China, the Communists possessed one of the greatest masses of disinherited human beings the world has ever seen. And because they found the key to the heart of these women, they also found one of the keys to victory over Chiang Kaishek."

But the peasants would never even have spoken up, no less made a revolution if Communist Party cadres had lorded it

over them like the bureaucrats of old. So Mao developed a new style of leadership — "the style of plain living and hard struggle." Cadres were to go to the villages, to live the harsh life of the peasants, and to earn their respect by learning from them and demonstrating new ways to them rather than trying to command them.

" 'Draw the bow without shooting, just indicate the motions.' It is for the peasants themselves to cast aside the idols . . . It is wrong for anybody to do it for them."
–Mao

IN THE MEANTIME, IN KMT AREAS, IT'S BUSINESS AS USUAL...

...even during the devastating Honan famine, as described by American Journalist Theodore White:

"The peasants, as we saw them, were dying. They were dying on the roads, in the mountains, by the railway stations, in their mud huts, in the fields. And as they died, the government continued to wring from them the last possible ounce of tax.

The government in county after county was demanding of the peasant more actual poundage of grain than he had raised on his acres. No excuses were allowed; peasants who were eating elm bark and dried leaves had to haul their last sack of seed grain to the tax collector's office. Peasants who were so weak they could barely walk had to collect fodder for the army's horses, fodder that was more nourishing that the filth they were cramming into their own mouths...

We knew that there was a fury, as cold and relentless as death itself, in the bosom of the peasants of Honan, that their loyalty had been hollowed to nothingness by the extortion of their government."

Mao summed it up. "The Kuomintang is an amorphous body of no definite character or program . . . Chiang is stubborn. But fundamentally he is a gangster."

YALTA

We've said it before, Stalin and his cohorts didn't believe in a Mao-style revolution in China.

"The Chinese are radish communists, red on the outside, white on the inside," said Foreign Minister Molotov.

In February 1945, F.D.R., uncle Joe Stalin and Winnie met in Yalta to divide up the new world.

THE WAR ENDS...

THE CIVIL WAR BEGINS...

At Yalta, China had been left in the U.S. sphere of influence. But Uncle Sam was getting nervous. While American negotiators scurried around trying to bring Mao and Chiang together, old Sam decided to lend a hand (or two or three or four) to poor, beleaguered Chiang. After all, China must in no way end up Communist!

Chiang's troops were rearmed with American weapons and a massive American airlift moved them all over China to help him reestablish control. Oh yes, 60,000 U.S. marines were landed in North China as a "force for stability." (We'll let you guess who the forces of instability were.)

Unfortunately, by 1949, almost all of China (and most of the American arms) were in Mao's hands.

So did Uncle Sam give up and recognize an independent China?

NOT BY A LONG SHOT!

For one thing, Chiang and his remaining troops ended up on the island of Taiwan (Formosa). Here, with U.S. help, he founded a phantom country, the "Republic of China". Also known as "Nationalist China".

IN THE following years, Uncle Sam tried awfully hard to quarantine China entirely. Are you surprised then that Mao "leaned to one side" in the onrushing Cold War. The Russian side, of course.

Europeans making a tactical withdrawal after Chiang's fall...

1ST OCTOBER 1949...

FROM the Celestial Peace entrance to the Imperial Palace of Peking, Mao Tsetung proclaimed the establishment of...

The People's Republic of China

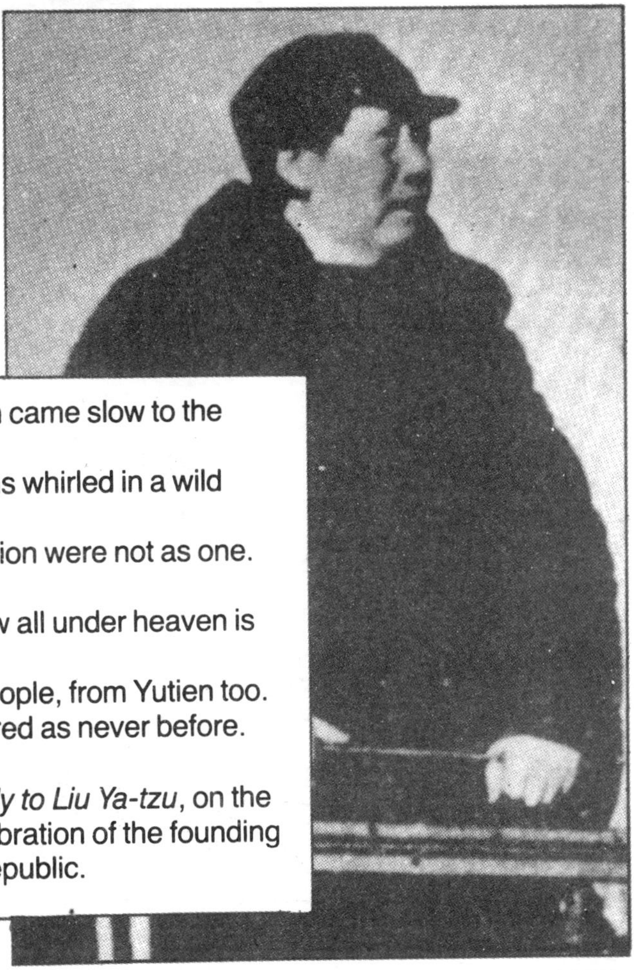

Night was long, dawn came slow to the
Crimson Land.
Centuries-old demons whirled in a wild
dance.
And five hundred million were not as one.

Now at the cock-crow all under heaven is
bright.
Music from all our people, from Yutien too.
And the poet is inspired as never before.

Mao's poem, *Reply to Liu Ya-tzu*, on the 1950 national celebration of the founding of the People's Republic.

THAT fellow Chiang Kaishek went—and with him went vice, corruption, foreign domination, slavery, war, hunger, parasites and war-lords.

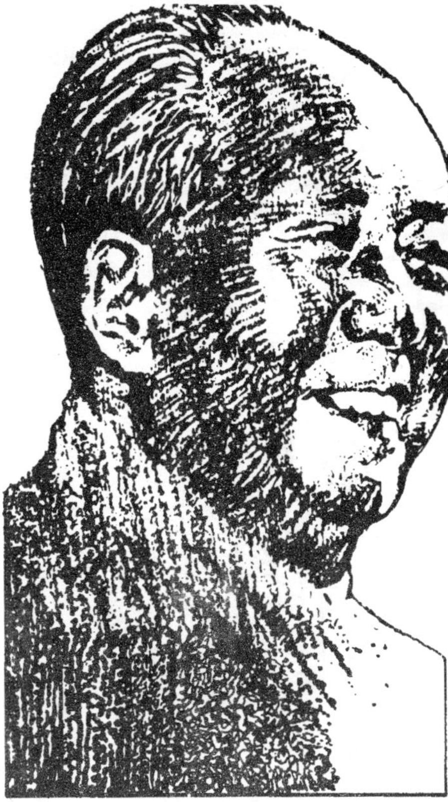

MAO was now 56 years old. He'd grown fatter. He'd written many things about philosophy, warfare and politics.

Mao was handed a RUINED country. Industry, agriculture, trade, everything devastated. In short, chaos!

Almost total illiteracy, disease, misery and hunger, high unemployment and the leftovers of vice, prostitution...

So, WHAT was Mao going to do to raise China from feudal backwardness?

FOR MAO, there was the example of Russia.

Russia, without capitalists, had become an advanced country. She had risen from a poor, backward country.

STALIN had backed Chiang Kaishek right to the end. But now he had to recognize political reality. He was the first to give official recognition to Chairman Mao's new government and invited him to Moscow.

Mao came back from this trip with aid from the Socialist giant. Soviet technicians, technology, an education programme and 300million dollars.

All of which the Chinese had to pay for.

VICTORY in the civil war had been so rapid that Mao and his comrades found themselves in control of China's cities, unprepared.

The economic and social disarray in the cities was unbelievable

They had to do something quick... but what?

The Soviet model

It seemed to offer a ready-made form of top-down organization. The Yanan experience was pushed aside.

"The Communist Party of the Soviet Union has built a great and splendid socialist state. It is our best teacher and we must learn from it."

Mao.

... runaway inflation was brought under control. Industry was nationalized and planned. Vast numbers of students were trained in the sciences, largely in Russia. New schools spread across the country. Factories were built with the help of Russian technicians.
So what was so wrong?
The peasants were being forgotten!
All the lessons of Yanan were being ignored!

STILL MAO WAS UNEASY...

"We had no experience, China had no experts, the minister of planning was himself an outsider, so we had to copy from foreign countries, and having copied we were unable to distinguish good from bad. We lacked understanding of the whole economic situation, and understood still less the economic differences between the Soviet Union and China. So all we could do was to follow blindly."

"I couldn't have eggs or chicken soup for three years because an article appeared in the Soviet Union which said that one shouldn't eat them. Later they said one could eat them. It didn't matter whether the article was correct or not, the Chinese listened all the same and respectfully obeyed. In short, the Soviet Union was tops."

Mao feared that the growing reliance on Russian-style heavy industrial and technological development, concentrated in a few big cities would aggravate the traditional gap between city and country. Socialism will never be achieved!

Nor could the Chinese do what Stalin had done — drain the existing surplus in the rural areas in order to develop industry. There was no surplus in China

In any case, said Mao, "The Russians have made grave mistakes in handling the peasants. . . . You want the hen to lay more eggs and yet you don't feed it, you want the horse to run fast, and yet you don't let it graze. What kind of logic is that?"

The answer? Raise productivity through a continuous revolutionary transformation of the countryside!

FROM the first days of the People's Republic, Mao had sought a far-reaching programme of land reform.

Nice idea, to give each peasant land. But that made an infinite number of tiny peasant farms – and little cooperative effort to tackle the poverty that condemned all the peasants.

New ways had to be found to work the land.

Painting by a peasant

RIDING roughshod over the objections of many of his colleagues, Mao supported the movement from private landholdings to mutual-aid teams, from lower to higher collectives, and finally to:

THE GREAT LEAP FORWARD

'Experiment in Everything'

With Mao's support, a tumultuous mass movement swept China in 1958. In the cities, attacks were launched against rigid, Soviet hierarchical methods of organization in industry and education. But it was in the countryside, out of the spontaneous radicalism of local rural leaders and poor peasants, that the greatest innovation came.

THE COMMUNES

were an audacious attempt to reverse the Soviet model, both economically and politically. What the peasant produced through intensified collective efforts was to go not to the city, but into the hands of the peasants themselves!

In Communes ranging in size up to 20,000 people, peasants would poo' their resources to develop locally needed industries.

Communes were to set up schools and small technical institutes as the first step in the marriage of modern science and traditional peasant agricultural wisdom. Rudimentary health clinics were to provide the basis for a frontal assault on the low level of rural health. Communal laundries and grain mills, increasing electrification, and new water projects would lighten some of the backbreaking chores of peasant existence.

At some future moment, the city and the countryside would blend into each other and become one!

Overjoyed by their "great leap" towards Communism, the Maoists began to disregard sound economic and Marxist considerations. They sought to advance faster than was possible, and the pent-up demands for radical change from the poor pushed them even further and faster than they had intended to go.

Soon the country was wracked by disasters — crop failures, industrial mismanagement, flood damage, drought.

Just in the midst of this perilous time, political differences between Russia and China became so acute that the USSR abruptly withdrew its technicians and assistance. Many factories ground to a halt.

"Three hard years" followed, 1959-1962, a time of retrenchment and consolidation. Sharp divisions now appeared in the Communist Party leadership — leading to the TWO LINE STRUGGLE

CRITICISM OF MAO FLEW EVERY WHICH WAY!

The Russians had a few choice words of their own: "The maoist cavalry-charge approach to economic growth can lead only to barracks socialism. Mao has reduced class struggle to the level of a tantrum thrown by the elemental forces of nature"

"[If the communes are allowed to perish] I will go to the countryside to lead the peasants to overthrow the government. If those of you in the Liberation Army won't follow me, then I will go and find a Red Army, and organize another Liberation Army. But I think the Liberation Army would follow me."

Mao

Hey, seriously now folks...

...Mao's argument basically was:

You are wrong to believe that the peasants want only a small plot of land and a bare existence. They are motivated by more than material self-interest. They are burning with a demand for change — AND IT IS OUT OF THIS PASSIONATE DEMAND THAT EVERYTHING IN OUR REVOLUTION HAS ULTIMATELY COME. You comrades fear this. You carp about peasant "excesses" and the "chaos" of mass movements. You feel more at home with bureaucratic methods — that curse of thousands of years of Chinese history. You fall back on the Soviet model to justify another bureaucratic way.

But socialism is not to be found down such a road. Let the peasants and workers become the masters of their own productive destiny, and they will produce. Let their energies be multiplied through co-operative efforts and a leadership deeply rooted in their midst, and they will break the grip of poverty. The Communes came out of an earthshaking mass movement — and despite the problems and hardships that came with them, they are a gateway to a better future.

As more and more of his lifelong colleagues turned against him, Mao began to re-examine everything. First he took another good, hard look at the Soviet Union.

KRUSHCHEV: We are the model for socialism. No more exploited classes exist in Russia. No more antagonistic contradictions between leaders and the people. No more need for mass struggle and conflict.

MAO: Who's kidding whom? Now that I think about it, the Russians aren't even socialists!

MAO MEANT THAT...

1. An irreconcilable and antagonistic class contradiction has emerged between the Soviet people and the privileged bureaucratic stratum.

2. A tiny number of bureaucrats are reaping high salaries, high rewards, and a great variety of personal subsidies. They are completely divorced from the working people.

3. Material incentives have been substituted for the socialist principles, "from each according to his ability, to each according to his work."

4. Stalin's basic error was mistrust of the peasants.

5. Stalin emphasized only technology. He wanted nothing but technology, nothing but cadre. No politics, no masses.

6 From start to finish of his book, *Economic Problems of Socialism in The USSR*, Stalin says nothing about human beings. He sees things, but not people.

MAO THEN TOOK A LONG HARD LOOK AT CHINA...

* ESPECIALLY WITHIN THE COMMUNIST PARTY

MAO ASKS:

After fifteen years in power, how are medical resources distributed to the people?

"Tell the Ministry of Public Health that it only works for fifteen percent of the total population of the country and that this fifteen percent is mainly composed of gentlemen, while the broad masses of the peasants do not get any medical treatment. First they don't have any doctors; second they don't have any medicine. The Ministry of Public

Health is not a Ministry of Public Health for the people, so why not change the name to the Ministry of Urban Health, the Ministry of Gentlemen's Health, or even to the Ministry of Urban Gentle-men's Health."

JUST LOOK HOW SMALL WOMEN HAVE BECOME:

"Of course, it was necessary to give women legal equality to begin with! But from there on, everything still remains to be done. The thought, culture, and customs which brought China to where we found her must disappear, and the thought, customs, and culture of proletarian China, which does not yet exist, must appear. The Chinese woman doesn't yet exist either, among the masses; but she is beginning to want to exist."

Mao to Malraux, 1965

AND AS FOR INTELLECTUALS

"Professors — we have been afraid of them ever since we came into the towns. We did not despise them, we were terrified of them. When confronted by people with piles of learning we felt that we were good for nothing. . . . Ever since ancient times the people who founded new schools of thought were all young people without too much learning. They had the ability to recognize new things at a glance and, having grasped them, they opened fire on the old fogeys. . . . Then those with learning oppressed them. Isn't that what history is like? When we started to make revolution, we were mere twenty-year old boys while the rulers of that time were old and experienced. They had more learning, but we had more truth."

TRUE KNOWLEDGE REQUIRES PRACTICAL EXPERIENCE!

"Confucius never attended middle school or university . . . Gorky had only two years of primary school; his learning was all self-taught. Franklin of America was originally a newspaper editor, yet he discovered electricity. Watt was a worker, yet he invented a steam engine."

Gorky (right) and Lu Hsun

"Among intellectuals, the question of world outlook often is symbolized by the way they look at knowledge. Some people consider knowledge as their own possession and wait to get a good price in the market."

SO WHAT DOES MAO CONCLUDE?

If the Chinese want socialism, they will have to fight for it. Socialism does not come naturally. There must be revolution on the political, ideological, and cultural fronts — not just the economic. Revolution must be — UNINTERRUPTED.

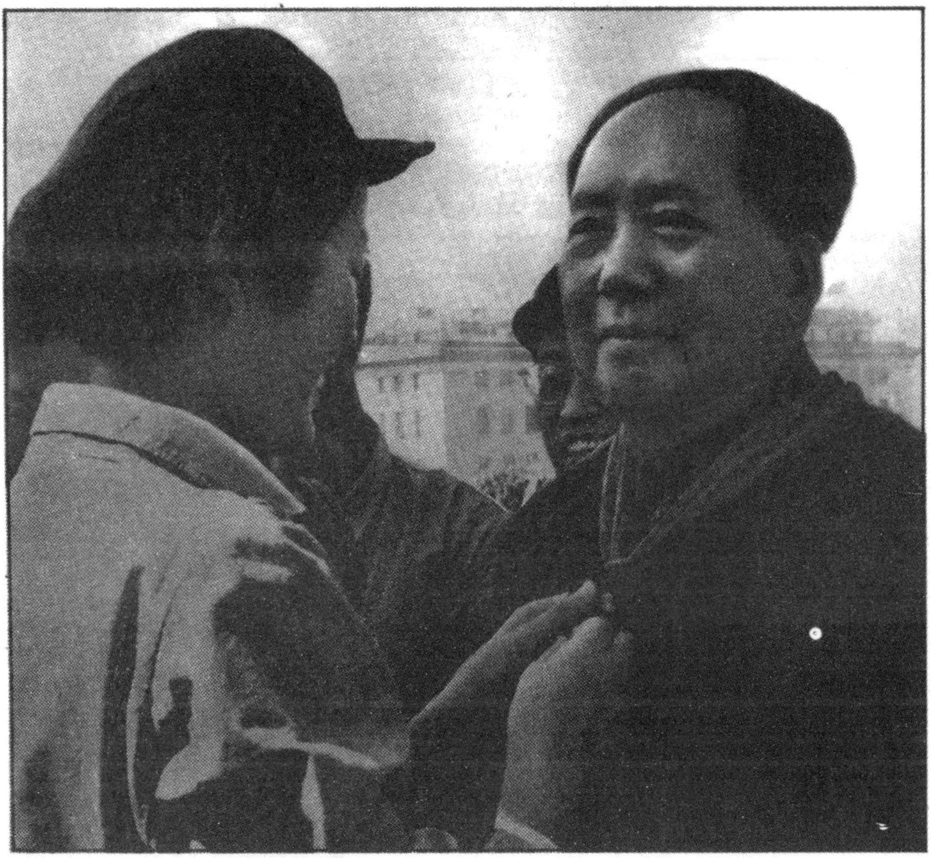

"Marxism consists of thousands of truths, but they all boil down to the one sentence, 'It is right to rebel.' For thousands of years, it had been said that it was right to oppress, it was right to exploit, and it was wrong to rebel. This old verdict was only reversed with the appearance of Marxism. This is a great contribution. It was through struggle that the proletariat learned this truth, and Marx drew the conclusion. And from this truth there follows resistance, struggle, the fight for socialism."

1966...

AND China gave the world—and Russia—something new to talk about.

In Peking a startling political movement began:

THE CULTURAL REVOLUTION

ENCOURAGED by Mao himself, millions of young Chinese thronged the streets. They came out to voice their discontent with, and criticism of, officials; of methods, of errors, deviations and abuses of power and privilege.

Thousands of DAZIBAOS – enormous hand-written posters – were slapped on public buildings and walls right across China.

Idealistic youngsters loudly denounced the elements of corruption.

"Revolutionaries are Monkey Kings, their magic omnipotent, for they possess Mao Tsetung's invincible thought. We wield our golden rods, display our supernatural powers, and use our magic to turn the old world upside down,

smash it to pieces, pulverize it, create chaos, and make a tremendous mess, the bigger the better! We must do this to the present revisionist middle school attached to the Tsinghua University, make a rebellion in a big way, rebel to the end! We are bent on creating a tremendous proletarian uproar and hewing out a proletarian new world."

UNIVERSITIES in China were all closed for nearly four years.

Everything was questioned.

In the factories, workers joined with the Red Guards, those irascible young people, and questioned work methods and their leaders.

Many, and very important, heads rolled. The President, Liu Shaoqi, was vilified and put under house arrest.

Lin Biao
Liu Shaoqi

THE Cultural Revolution aimed to root out everything left of the old order.

Followers of the Soviet line or of capitalism were in trouble.

For the moment.

THE CULTURAL REVOLUTI AS MAO SAW IT...

FIRST, Mao wanted to create a New Society in which people perform social functions for the satisfaction derived from contributing to a new ideal.

Human beings without egotism, vices, vile thoughts, unselfish, modest.

Sounds like pure Utopia?

SECOND, Mao attacked the "capitalist roaders."

"Capitalist roaders are power-holders who follow the capitalist road. During the democratic revolution they took an active part in the fight against the three big mountains. But in the fight against the bourgeoisie after the nationwide liberation, they were not so enthusiastic. They actively took part in the war against local tyrants and in the redistribution of land, but they were not so enthusiastic when it came to collectivization of farming after the nationwide liberation. They do not take the socialist road, but they now hold power."

Mao had become a god for the Chinese. Only he was right. Not to think like him meant ending up an enemy of the people!

ON HAD TWO PURPOSES,

Apart from criticism and destruction, what came out of the Cultural Revolution? A greater industrial democracy, with workers participating in the running of their factories and managers forced to work on the shop floor regularly so they could feel what it was like. People working in offices went regularly to the countryside to "learn from the peasants". University courses were shortened – less theory, more practice. Doctors left their expensive city hospitals to go out to the countryside to train "barefoot doctors" who would care for the sick in remote villages.

MAO'S Red Guards had toppled Liu Shaoqi. The way was open for a successor. Lin Biao, one of the great heroes of the revolutionary war, was seen constantly at Mao's side. (He was the one who compiled Mao's famous Little Red Book.) Soon he became the most outspoken advocate of the Mao cult. Now (1970), Mao was 77!

THEN, in 1971, just when it seemed like everything was going his way, Lin Biao died mysteriously. It was suddenly announced that a plane taking him to Moscow, after an abortive anti-Mao coup d'etat, had crashed.

That's the official version anyway!

A NEW group of leaders emerged at the end of the Cultural Revolution. Zhang Chunqiao, Wang Hongwen, Yao Wenyuan and Mao's last wife, Jiang Quing.

Their influence grew because Mao was ill and old and less active than he had been.

Jiang Quing · Zhang Chunqiao · Yao Wenyuan · Wang Hongwen

This new group of leaders (now known as the Gang of Four) were convinced that the Chinese had been wrong in the '50s to allow the continuation of the old cultural traditions. During the Cultural Revolution these traditions, and their protagonists, writers, dancers, Peking Opera performers, scholars, had all been attacked.

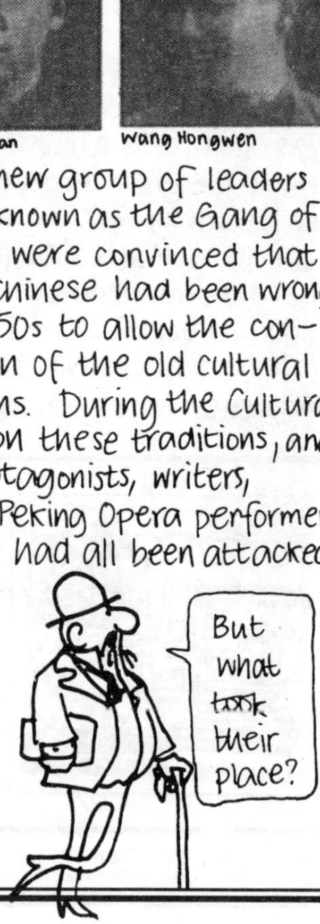

Modern Revolutionary Operas

These had to have very perfect heroes for the public to admire — and very wicked villains who couldn't possibly be confused with the heroes! The Party had to play a leading role, of course!

Not many were made, since the conditions were hard to fulfill.

In life, as in these operas, people were expected to be very idealistic and always put politics in command. No question of financial incentives. Workers worked harder for political and moral rewards.

Newspapers didn't carry news — but articles written by Zhang Chunqiao and Yao Wenyuan which exhorted: "Overthrow the rightist revisionist wind on the educational front", "Put politics in command", "Fear neither hardship nor death in serving the people". Very famous was, "Criticize Lin Biao and Confucius".

What did the people feel about all this?

There were signs that the people were not happy. There were riots in Peking and many other cities in April 1976. These were provoked by the Gang of Four's refusal to let the people commemorate Chou Enlai at the Qing-ming Festival when the Chinese traditionally honor their dead and feed the hungry ancestral ghosts.

ON September 9th, 1976, Mao Tsetung died in Peking. He was a mere 83 years old.

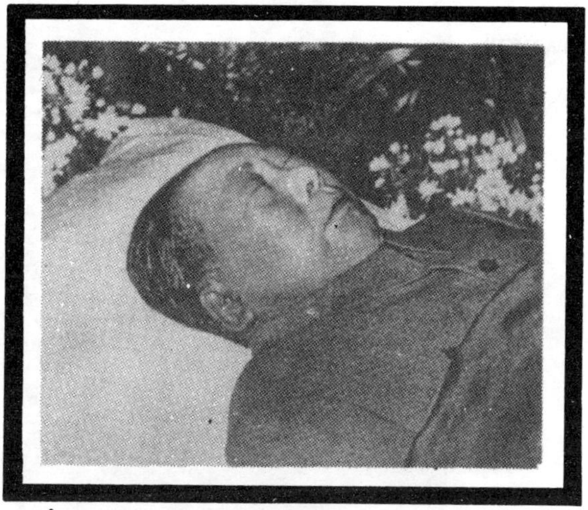

(One of his last wishes was to be cremated, but he was out of luck...)

Though Mao had personally designated his successor, Hua Guofeng,...

Hua Guofeng moved quickly and overthrew the Gang of Four. The people certainly showed their feelings then! They say that all the wine in the shops was sold out as people held parties to celebrate the downfall of the Four.

Chairman Hua Guofeng

Gang of Four in effigy

With Deng Xiaoping, Hua Guofeng started a program of modernization and reversal — bringing back things overthrown and criticized during the Cultural Revolution.

Deng Xiaoping

CAN anyone understand all these reversals, downfalls and rises to power?

Take Deng Xiaoping.

He was twice disgraced by Mao himself, but rose a third time to an important government post.
Every cloud has a silver lining..!

Do you think you can spot DENG XIAOPING and HUA GUOFENG in this caricature which satirized them and their party followers?

Could even Mao have made sense of it all? He certainly worried about what would happen after his death . . .

"Perhaps the right wing will seize power after my death. If they do this, then they will have a surprise. Since 1911, when the emperor was overthrown, a reactionary regime has not been able to hold China for long. If there is a right-wing, anti-communist coup d'etat in China, then I am certain that those elements will not know a moment of peace.

It is very possible that they will be able to retain their dominance for a while. If the Right wing seizes power, it will be able to use my words to retain power for a time. But the Left will use other quotations of mine, and organize themselves, and overthrow the Right wing."

And he offered one final warning. . . .

"You are making the socialist revolution, and yet you don't know where the bourgeoisie is. It is right in the Communist Party — those in power taking the capitalist road."

What about the Gang of Four? Do we really know what they represented? They rose to power in the Cultural Revolution and were associated with its ideas: such as overthrowing the bourgeois rights of senior officials.

But they have been accused of committing the same sins they attacked in others! Madam Mao – Jiang Quing – liked to wear smart clothes and watch the films she forbade to others.

A satire of the "Empress" Jiang Quing

Recent Chinese foreign policy doesn't make it any clearer!

Once upon a time, they lambasted Krushchev for his policy of "peaceful coexistence" with the U.S. Then Nixon Coca Cola, and American military delegations were in Peking.

Once they loudly supported people's revolutionary movements throughout the world. And then China supported Pinochet in Chile, the mercenaries against Angola etc, etc!

THE author admits he's as puzzled as everyone else about the direction China will now take.
Only one thing is sure. Nobody can deny what Mao Tsetung has done for the Chinese people.
The best tribute to Mao's memory is that the Chinese people mourned his death like the death of a father.
MAO
HIS BOOK

The Pinyin system

Chinese is not an alphabetic language. But for westeners who cannot read characters, it can be spelled out in the Roman alphabet. Each European country had its own system of romanization. The one most commonly used in England and the United States was called the Wade-Giles system (after the two men who worked it out). China developed a Chinese system of romanization called *pinyin*, which means 'to phoneticize'. From January 1st, 1979, all works published in China which use romanization use the pinyin system. The major newspapers and press agencies of the world have followed the Chinese and replaced Wade-Giles and all other systems with Pinyin.

The sound values of pinyin have to be learnt before the system can be used properly. The most difficult letters in pinyin are x, q, z and zh. X is a hiss, halfway between the s and sh; q is like the 'chee' in 'cheese'; z is like the z in zebra; and zh is like a j as in jump or juggle. When you have learnt these, you will find that pinyin is a better (more accurate) system than Wade-Giles. Some of the changes you may notice in this book are in the names of people like Zhu De (formerly Chu Te) whose name is pronounced 'Jew Der', or the Qianlong emperor (formerly Ch'ien-lung) whose name should be pronounced Chee-en long

Our use of pinyin in this book is not consistent. The best-known names have been left in the old familiar system because that is how you will see them still in other reference books. For instance Chou Enlai in pinyin should be Zhou Enlai; Kuomintang should be spelled in pinyin Guomindang. Even the Chinese themselves exclude the capital, Peking (Beijing in pinyin) from the pinyin system, probably because 'Peking' is too familiar.

Similarly, Chiang Kaishek (usually seen as Kai-shek) and Sun Yatsen (Yat-sen) are widely known by their names which do not fit into the standard romanization of *putonghua* (common speech) but are romanized from the Cantonese dialect. Chiang Kaishek in standard pinyin romanization would be Jiang Jieshi; Sun Yatsen would be Sun Zhongshan.

Books on Mao and the Revolution

MAO TSETUNG, Poems and Selected Works (5 volumes) are both available from Foreign Languages Press, Peking.

MAO TSETUNG, A Critique of Soviet Economics, Monthly Review Press, New York, 1977.

Jack Belden, China Shakes the World, Monthly Review Press, New York, 1970; Barrie & Jenkins, London, 1972

Jean Chesneaux, The People's Republic of China, 1949-1976, Pantheon, New York, 1979

Jean Chesneaux, Marianna Bastid, Marie-Claire Bergère, China: From the Opium Wars to the 1911 Revolution, Volume 1, and From the 1911 Revolution to Liberation, Volume 2, Pantheon, New York, 1976, 1977.

Jacques Guillermaz, History of the Chinese Communist Party, 1921-1949, Methuen, London, 1972.

Jacques Guillermaz, The Chinese Communist Party in Power, 1949-1976, Dawson, Folkestone, 1976; Westview, New York, 1976.

William Hinton, Fanshen: A Documentary of Revolution in a Chinese Village, Vintage, New York, 1968; Penguin, London, 1972

David Milton & Nancy Dall Milton, The Wind Will Not Subside, Pantheon, New York, 1976.

David Milton, Nancy Milton and Franz Schurmann, People's China, Vintage, 1974.

Robert Payne, Portrait of a Revolutionary: Mao Tsetung, Abelard-Schuman, New York, 1961

Stuart Schram, Mao Tsetung, Penguin, New York, 1968; Penguin, London, 1967.

Stuart Schram, Chairman Mao Talks to the People, Pantheon, 1975; U.K. edition: Mao Tsetung Unrehearsed, Penguin, London, 1974

Edgar Snow, Red Star Over China, Bantam, New York, 1978; Penguin, London, 1972

Edgar Snow, The Long Revolution, Vintage, New York, 1973, U.K. edition: China's Long Revolution, Penguin, London, 1974